Table of conte

Welcome, Anglers

Every year we do it. It has become a tradition.

When it's the third week of April, off we go, 21 of us.

We go to Watts Bar Lake in Tennessee and fish like maniacs, daylight to dark, for seven days or longer. Fish, fish, fish.

What a great group of fellows! We have a good time!

But if we were to rate the fishing honestly, I think we would agree a lot more fish could be caught if we remained in Ohio and fished the waters we know best.

When it comes to fishing, we have a lot going for us in this state. If you know what's available, where to find it and when to get there, you can be a successful angler.

That's what we try to point out in the Ohio Fishing Guide. We search for the what, where and the when to help you and your friends have a better year with rod and reel.

Widely known is Lake Erie's reputation as the "walleye capital of the world." We can assure you that reputation will continue.

Moreover, you can count on some of the greatest smallmouth bass fishing at

Lake Erie in the next few years and you will see the yellow perch population come roaring back. In a couple of years it will remind you of the good old days of perch fishing.

Less known to some anglers are developments at inland lakes and on the Ohio River. We're calling Indian Lake the "saugeye capital of the world" and don't think it's an exaggeration.

After all, Ohio is the world leader in production of the saugeye and this hybrid fish at Indian Lake often yields limit catches before the lake freezes, through the ice, after the ice breaks up and during the spring.

Coming on rapidly in the northwest sector is unrivaled steelhead fishing at four rivers flowing into Lake Erie. The upground reservoirs in northwest Ohio are more productive than ever.

All along the Ohio River, fishing has improved because the water quality is better. Moreover, at nearly every inland lake in Ohio, bass fishing is more desirable because length limits have been set according to the needs of each body of water.

Fishing has become a year around recreation for many people in Ohio. You also may have noticed more people fishing at night during the summer.

The wildlife division has enlarged its catfish operation to include stocking of channel catfish on alternate years at a number of lakes. At some of these lakes, the summer creel census has found that almost as many people fish at night as during the day.

When I go crappie fishing with my buddies, they often accuse me of pulling in catfish behind their back. I admit to nothing, except to say it's getting harder to leave Ohio.

We hope it will be for you,

Young fisherman approves of Dow Lake Trout Festival.

Special Thanks

The author thanks the Division of Wildlife and the Ohio Department of Natural Resources for the many materials provided in this book, including fishing maps.

Division of Wildlife fish management supervisors, and their assistants, offered invaluable assistance, as did other state personnel and individual anglers who shared information about fishing.

The author is grateful to Ms. Jan Krause, director of Cox Custom Publishing, for her enthusiastic support of this publishing venture.

And, last but by no means least, thanks to Donna Robey for countless hours of painstaking proof reading.

The Ohio Fishing Guide

All photos by Jim Robey except where noted.

Three Jims ...

Robey

Morris

Guenthner

Jim Robey grew up in Columbus, went to South High School and majored in wildlife conservation at Ohio State University. A second generation outdoor writer, Robey fished with his dad and brother, George Robey I and II, from Lake Erie to the Ohio River, plus the rivers and lakes between.

Jim joined the staff of *The Journal Herald*, later to merge with the *Dayton Daily News*, as outdoor writer in 1963. He retired as a staff reporter in 1993 and continues to write his column and gather information for the *Ohio Fishing Guide.*

Jim Morris caught his first porgy at the age of five and he's been fishing ever since. A native of Connecticut, he spent the next 10 years as a saltwater fishermen, then moved to Ohio and found out a largemouth wasn't some wise guy in study hall.

He is the former executive editor of the *Troy Daily News* , has been the *Dayton Daily News* outdoor writer since March of 1994 and is a member of the Outdoor Writers of Ohio.

He and his wife, Pat, live in Troy and have two grown children, Laura and Jim. He caught his first muskie at the age of 51, last year.

Jim Guenthner was born in Miami County and moved to St. Petersburg, Fla. at the tender age of two. He spent the next six years fishing in Tampa Bay with his dad Jim, and his grandad, where he developed an enthusiasm for the outdoors.

When the family moved back to Miami County, Jim happily fished the Great Miami River and the lakes, ponds and old Miami-Erie Canal feeder around Piqua.

Jim and his wife, Carolyn have two sons in college. He has been employed at the *Dayton Daily News* as a graphic designer since 1970.

Condensed Fishing Regulations

Resident fishing licenses are for persons age 16 through 65 who have resided in Ohio for at least six months just prior to applying for a license. The cost is $15, including a $1 writing fee.

An annual non-resident fishing license costs $24, including the writing fee.

Ohio has a 3-day non-resident tourist license for $15.

Fishing licenses for residents who are 66 years of age or older are available free from the Division of Wildlife. Under certain conditions, exemptions may apply to landowners fishing private property, their guests, physically handicapped and U.S. Armed Forces personnel.

Most fishing is unlimited by season, but size and bag limits now apply to one or more species at nearly every public body of water.

Under the wildlife division's intensely managed operation, the size limit on bass may be adjusted from one year to the next. Size limits also apply to walleyes, trout, hybrid striped bass, striped bass and muskellunge at different lakes.

In the lake section of this guide, you will find size and creel limits mentioned with respect to each reservoir, but always cross-check the information with the official digest of fishing regulations.

When buying your license, ask for the booklet of Ohio Fishing Regulations, or write: Division of Wildlife, 1840 Belcher Drive, Fountain Square, Columbus, OH 43224.

Photo by Bill Reinke

When water temperature rises to 44°, or higher, spring walleye anglers wade into the Maumee River.

5

Who to call for fishing information

MAIN OFFICE
Fish Management Section
Ohio Division of Wildlife
1840 Belcher Drive,
Fountain Square
Columbus, Ohio 43224
(614) 265-6345
1-800-WILDLIFE

CENTRAL OHIO
★ **District One**
1500 Dublin Road
Columbus, Ohio 43215
(614) 644-3925

NORTHWEST OHIO
★ **District Two**
952 Lima Avenue
Box A
Findlay, Ohio 45840
(419) 424-5000

NORTHEAST OHIO
★ **District Three**
912 Portage Lakes Drive
Akron, Ohio 44319
(330) 644-2293

SOUTHEAST OHIO
★ **District Four**
360 E. State Street
Athens, Ohio 45701
(614) 594-2211

SOUTHWEST OHIO
★ **District Five**
1076 Old Springfield Pike
Box 576
Xenia, Ohio 45385
(937) 372-9261

INLAND FISH RESEARCH UNIT
10517 Canal Rd. SE
Hebron, Ohio 43025
614-928-7034

TIP PROGRAM
Turn-in-a-Poacher
1840 Belcher Drive
Fountain Square
Columbus, Ohio 43224
Toll-Free 1-800-POACHER

LICENSE SECTION
1840 Belcher Drive
Fountain Square
Columbus, Ohio 43224
614-265-7037

OHIO RIVER COORDINATOR
1840 Belcher Drive,
Fountain Square,
Columbus, Ohio 43224
(614) 265-6343

LAKE ERIE ENFORCEMENT UNIT
P.O. BOX 650
305 E. Shoreline Dr.
Sandusky, Ohio 44870
(419) 625-8062

LAKE ERIE FISH RESEARCH UNIT
P.O. Box 650
Ohio Fisheries Bldg.
Sandusky, Ohio 44870
(419) 625-8062

FAIRPORT HARBOR
FISH RESEARCH UNIT
421 High Street
Fairport Harbor, Ohio 44097
216-352-6100

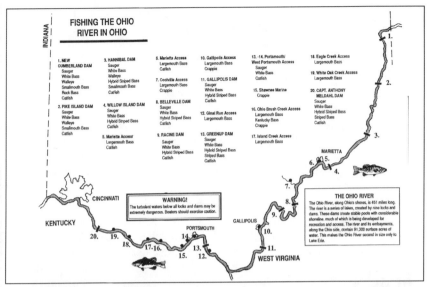

FISHING THE OHIO
RIVER IN OHIO

INDIANA

1. NEW
CUMBERLAND DAM
Sauger
White Bass
Walleye
Smallmouth Bass
Rock Bass
Catfish

2. PIKE ISLAND DAM
Sauger
White Bass
Walleye
Smallmouth Bass
Catfish

3. HANNIBAL DAM
Sauger
White Bass
Walleye
Smallmouth Bass
Catfish

4. WILLOW ISLAND DAM
Sauger
White Bass
Hybrid Striped Bass
Catfish

5. Marietta Access
Largemouth Bass
Catfish

6. Marietta Access
Largemouth Bass
Catfish

7. Coolville Access
Largemouth Bass
Crappie

8. BELLEVILLE DAM
Sauger
White Bass
Hybrid Striped Bass
Catfish

9. RACINE DAM
Sauger
White Bass
Hybrid Striped Bass
Catfish

10. Gallipolis Access
Largemouth Bass
Crappie

11. GALLIPOLIS DAM
Sauger
White Bass
Hybrid Striped Bass
Catfish

12. Ginal Run Access
Largemouth Bass

13. GREENUP DAM
Sauger
White Bass
Hybrid Striped Bass
Striped Bass
Catfish

13. -14. Portsmouth/
West Portsmouth Access
Sauger
White Bass
Catfish

15. Shawnee Marina
Crappie

16. Ohio Brush Creek Access
Largemouth Bass
Kentucky Bass
Crappie

17. Island Creek Access
Largemouth Bass

18. Eagle Creek Access
Largemouth Bass

19. White Oak Creek Access
Largemouth Bass

20. CAPT. ANTHONY
MELDAHL DAM
Sauger
White Bass
Hybrid Striped Bass
Striped Bass
Catfish

CINCINNATI

WARNING!
The turbulent waters below all locks and dams may be
extremely dangerous. Boaters should exercise caution.

KENTUCKY

20. 19.
18. 17. 16. 15. 12. 13.
PORTSMOUTH
14.

GALLIPOLIS

MARIETTA

THE OHIO RIVER
The Ohio River, along Ohio's shores, is 451 miles long.
The river is a series of lakes, created by nine locks and
dams. These dams create stable pools with considerable
shoreline, much of which is being developed for
recreation and access. The river and its embayments,
along the Ohio side, contain 91,300 surface acres of
water. This makes the Ohio River second in size only to
Lake Erie.

WEST VIRGINIA

Ohio River Improves

By Jim Robey

Water quality improvements over a 10-year period on the Ohio River have created a new "fishing frontier" along the eastern and southern border of Ohio, according to the Ohio Division of Wildlife.

The division says 80 different species of fish can be found in the 451 miles of river and the 91,300 acres of water available for fishing.

Nine navigational locks and dams along Ohio's portion of the river have formed lake-like pools with miles of shoreline to fish, plus bays and tributary streams.

Some of the best fishing is found in the fast-water below the dams where anglers take thousands of saugers, white bass, hybrid striped bass and other species of fish.

"Our surveys show the Ohio River is under utilized for fishing," says Scott Schell, aquatic biologist, Ohio Division of Wildlife.

Schell wrote the report on a five-year research project that was completed in 1993 in which comparisons were drawn between sport fishing in the Ohio River at that time of the study and a survey period 10 years earlier.

Participants of the $400,000 study included West Virginia, Kentucky, Indiana, the Ohio Division of Watercraft and the Division of Wildlife.

Besides writing the report, Schell spent most of his working hours on the Ohio River in 1992 and '93. He, along with others involved in the project, conducted 28,683 angler interviews representing 50,596 Ohio River anglers. Total fishing all along the river was estimated to be 2.5 million angler hours for both survey years.

With such a large number of interviews along the entire river and its bays, the biologists are confident they have a fairly accurate count of the number and types of fish taken by anglers during the survey period. This is what they learned:

Ohio River Fish Taken by Anglers 1992-93

BLACK BASS - 382,436. Of these, 58 percent were smallmouth bass, 37 percent were largemouth and 5 percent were spotted bass.

SAUGER AND WALLEYE - 858,789. Of these, 95.6 percent were sauger and 4.4 percent were walleye.

OTHER BASSES - 1,356,307 fish. Of these, 62 percent were white bass, 37 percent were hybrid striped bass and 1 percent were striped bass.

CATFISH - 135,232. Of these, 81 percent were channel catfish and 19 percent were flathead catfish.

If Ohio River fishing is under utilized, a similar survey taken last year and this one probably would find sport anglers are catching even more fish.

Surely the number of hybrid striped bass must be increasing because the Division of Wildlife is stocking this fish every year below each of the river dams at a rate of 10 hybrids per acre. Other states along the Ohio River also stock hybrid striped bass.

Biologists were able to draw the best comparison on fishing between the recent survey period and one 10 years previous with data collected at the section of the river shared by Ohio and West Virginia.

Here it was found that total fishing pressure over 10 years increased 225 percent. Of all boats on the Ohio River, the number used for fishing increased from 25 percent to 40 percent. And the length of the average fishing trip increased from 2.2 hours to 3 hours, a

sure sign the anglers are having more fun.

Schell said the Ohio River study pointed out further that many anglers still feel uncomfortable about eating the fish they catch, despite improvements in water quality.

Of all the bass taken, only 9 percent of them were kept. The others were released. Although most tournament anglers are in the habit of releasing fish, many non-tournament fishermen enjoy having fish for dinner.

Even the sauger and walleye anglers released all but 11 percent of the fish they caught, according to the study.

White bass and hybrid striped bass fishermen kept more of their fish. They took home 14.6 percent of their catch.

Schell said he was surprised to see so many people keeping catfish - 32.4 percent. "The closer we were to Cincinnati the more people we found who kept catfish," Schell stated.

The official state advisory on eating fish from the Ohio Department of Health says this for the Ohio River: "Channel catfish, carp - Do not eat. Flathead catfish - 6 meals a year."

As for bass and sauger in the Ohio River, the advisory recommends eating no more than one meal a week, or 52 a year. That, by the way, is exactly what is suggested for Lake Erie anglers who catch walleye and sheepshead.

The estimates on number of fish caught, as reported in the Ohio River survey, are conservative. Sauger anglers were not interviewed in mid-winter when they record their best catches.

All contacts with anglers were made during daylight hours. People who fish for catfish during the summer enjoy their best fishing at night.

(Continued on page 156)

Lake Erie-Ohio River ramps

Lake Erie Access

Area	County	Ramps	HP
Ashtabula Township Park SR 11, Ashtabula	Ashtabula	Yes	U
Beaver Park Ramp Lorain	Lorain	Yes	U
Catawba Island State Park SR 53 & 357, Port Clinton	Ottawa	Yes	U
City of Conneaut Public Docks Conneaut	Ashtabula	Yes	U
Cooley Creek County Ramp Near Oregon on Maumee Bay	Lucas	Yes	U
Cullen Municipal Park Summit & 101 St., Toledo	Lucas	Yes	U
East Battery Municipal Park Water & Meigs St., Sandusky	Sandusky	Yes (fee)	U
East 55th Street Municipal Marina Foot of E. 55th St., Cleveland	Cuyahoga	No	U
East Harbor State Park SR 163 & 269, Port Clinton	Ottawa	Yes	U
Edgewater Municipal Park Edgewater Dr., Cleveland	Cuyahoga	Yes	U
Fairport Boat Landing Water St., Fairport	Lake	Yes (fee)	U
Geneva-On-The-Lake SR 534, Village of Geneva-on-the-Lake	Ashtabula	Yes	U
Gordon Municipal Park E. 72 St., Cleveland	Cuyahoga	Yes	U
Green Harbor SR 53, Sandusky	Sandusky	Yes	U
Huron Municipal Boat Basin Foot of Main St., Huron	Erie	No	U
Huron River Marine Huron	Erie	Yes (fee)	U
Jack's Automarine SR 531, Ashtabula Harbor	Ashtabula	Yes (fee)	U
Jack's Marina Lorain	Lorain	Yes	U
Kelley's Island State Park Lake Erie, Port Clinton	Erie	No	U
Lakeshore Marina Eastlake	Lake	Yes (fee)	U
Little Portage River Access SR 53, five miles west of Port Clinton	Ottawa	Yes	U
Lorain City Ramp Lorain	Lorain	Yes	U
Lucas County Ramp Anchor Point	Lucas	Yes	U
Madison Township Boat Launch N. Perry	Lake	Yes	U
Marina Del Rio Ashtabula	Ashtabula	Yes (fee)	U
Ottawa County Ramp Catawba	Ottawa	Yes	U

9

Area	County	Ramps	HP
Pleasure Acres Toussaint	Ottawa	Yes	U
Portage River Access SR 2, 17 miles W. of Port Clinton	Ottawa	Yes	U
Port Clinton Wildlife Ramp Port Clinton	Ottawa	Yes	U
Put-In-Bay Public Docks East end of Island Park, Village of Put-In-Bay, South Bass Island	Ottawa	No	U
Rocky River Reservation Below the Rocky River bridge, Cleveland Metro. Park District	Cuyahoga	Yes (fee)	U
Rossford Marina On Maumee River in Rossford	Lucas	Yes	
Rutherford's Landing SR 283, Grand River	Lake	Yes (fee)	U
South Bass Island State Park West End of Island	Ottawa	Yes	U
Tibble's East Harbor East Harbor	Ottawa	Yes	U
Turtle Creek (Magee Marsh) Route 2, 17 miles W. of Port Clinton	Ottawa	Yes	U
Walbridge Municipal Park E. Broadway, Toledo	Lucas	Yes	U
Wards Canal (Metzger Marsh) Off SR 2, one mile E. of Bono	Lucas	Yes	U
West Harbor Public Boat Launch Port Clinton	Ottawa	Yes	U
White's Landing Sandusky Bay, Sandusky	Sandusky	Yes	U
Wildwood Park Neff Road, Cleveland	Cuyahoga	Yes (fee)	U

Ohio River Access

	County	Ramps	HP
Coolville Public Access Coolville	Athens	Yes	U
Eagle Creek ¼ mile E. of Ripley	Brown	Yes	U
Gallipolis Public Access S. end of First Ave.	Gallia	Yes	U
Ginat Run E. edge of Franklin Furnace, Braunlin Rd.	Scioto	Yes	U
Indian Guyan Creek 3 miles E. of Chesapeake	Lawrence	Yes	U
Indian Short Creek Public Ramp SR 7, S. of Warrington	Jefferson	Yes	U
Island Creek Public Access ½ mile E. of Manchester on US 52	Adams	Yes	U
Island Creek Ramp 5 miles N. of Steubenville	Jefferson	Yes	U
Marietta Public Access .Corner Fourth & Green St.	Washington	No	U
Marietta Public Access Mile 1.7 on Muskingum River	Washington	Yes	U
Miami Boat Ramp River Rd., S. of Cleves	Hamilton	Yes	U
Middleport Public Access SR 7, Middleport	Meigs	Yes	U

Area	County	Ramps	HP
Ohio Brush Creek 3.5 miles W. of Rome	Adams	Yes	U
Old Lock and Dam 27 3 miles W. of Proctorville	Lawrence	Yes	U
Pomeroy Public Access Main St., Pomeroy	Meigs	Yes	U
Portsmouth Public Access Foot of Court St., Portsmouth	Scioto	Yes	U
Riverside Park Riverside and South Side Ave., Cincinnati	Hamilton	Yes	U
Riverview Park Foot of Railroad St., Ironton	Lawrence	Yes	U
Schmidt Playground Kellog Ave., Cincinnati	Hamilton	Yes	U
Shawnee Marina West of Friendship	Scioto	Yes	U
Steubenville Public Ramp Corner Market & Water, Steubenville	Jefferson	Yes	U
Symmes Creek SR 7 E. of Chesapeake	Lawrence	Yes	U
Wellsville Public Ramp Corner 18th & Nevada St., Wellsville	Columbiana	Yes	U
White Oak Creek ½ mile E. of Higginsport	Brown	Yes	U

ODNR photo

White bass is one of the most abundant sport fish found in the Ohio River.

Ohio Public Fishing Areas

Legend

E — *Electric motors only*
U — *Unlimited horsepower*
No — *No motors permitted*
* — *10 mph on odd numbered days, U on even days*
MWCD — *Muskingum Watershed Conservancy District*

Section of state	Lake	Acreage	Location	Ramp	Max. HP
SW	Acton Lake	625	SR 732 & 177, 5 mi NW of Oxford	Yes	10
SW	Adams Lake	47	1 mi. NE of West Union on SR 41	No	E
C	Alum Creek Lake State Park	3,387	1 mi. W of I-71 on US 36 & SR 37	Yes	U
NE	Atwood Lake — MWCD	1,540	SR 212, 2 mi. S of New Cumberland	Yes	25
SE	Barkcamp State Park	117	1 mi. E of Belmont	Yes	E
SE	Barnesville Reservoir	98	3½ mi. S on SR 800, SW approx. 1½ mi. off Co. Rd. 514	No	E
NE	Beach City Wildlife Area — MWCD	420	SR 93, 1 mi. S of Beach City	No	10
NW	Beaver Creek Reservoir	110	5 mi. SW of Clyde, off SR 101	Yes	E
NE	Berlin Lake Wildlife Area	3,590	On SR 224 N of Alliance	Yes	U
NW	Bresler Reservoir	582	6 mi. W of Lima, off SR 81 on Kemp Rd.	Yes	E
C	Buckeye Lake State Park	3,800	SR 79, S of Hebron	Yes	U
SE	Burr Oak State Park	664	SR 13 & SR 78 NE of Glouster	Yes	10
SW	Caesar Creek	2,830	SR 73, 4½ mi. E of Waynesville	Yes	U
NE	Charles Mill Lake — MWCD	1,350	SR 603 & US 30 near Mifflin (Black Fork Creek)	Yes	10
SW	C.J. Brown Reservoir	2,120	1 mi. N of Springfield near SR 4	Yes	U
SW	Clark Lake Wildlife Area	100	2 mi. NE of Harmony off US 40	Yes	E
NE	Clear Fork Reservoir	977	SR 97 & SR 314 NW of Lexington (Clear Fork Creek)	Yes	10 mph
NE	Clendening Lake — MWCD	1,800	SR 8 at Tippecanoe	Yes	10
SE	Cowan State Park	692	SR 350, 2 mi. E of Clarksville	Yes	10
NE	Dale Walborn Reservoir	840	3½ mi. NW of Alliance, Price Rd.	Yes	6
NE	Deer Creek Reservoir	314	SR 183 at Limaville & NW of SR 225	Yes	E
C	Deer Creek Lake	1,277	SR 207 at Pancoastburg	Yes	U
C	Delaware State Park & Wildlife Area	1,330	8 mi. N of Delaware and E of US 23 (Olentangy River)	Yes	U
SE	Dillon State Park & Wildlife Area	1,560	On SR 146, 4 mi. NW of Zanesville (Licking River)	Yes	U
NE	East Branch Reservoir	416	SR 322 E of Claridon	Yes	E
SW	East Fork Lake	2,160	Off SR 222, 4 mi. SE of Batavia	Yes	U

12

Section of state	Lake	Acreage	Location	Ramp	Max. HP
			*10 hp odd days U even days		
SW	Eastwood Lake	190	SR 4, NE edge of Dayton (Mad River)	Yes	*
SW	Englewood Dam	70	Near SR 440 & Englewood (Stillwater River)	Yes	No
NW	Ferguson Reservoir	304	2 mi. E of Lima on High Street Rd.	No	E
NW	Findlay Reservoir 1	180	3 mi. SE of Findlay off SR 37	Yes	E
NW	Findlay Reservoir 2	827	3 mi. SE of Findlay off SR 37	Yes	10
NE	Findley State Park	93	SR 58, 2 mi. S of Wellington	Yes	E
SE	Forked Run State Park	104	On SR 124 W of Reedsville	Yes	10
SW	Grand Lake St. Marys State Park	12,500	SR 29, 2 mi. W of St. Marys	Yes	U
SW	Grant Lake Wildlife Area	181	SR 68, 3 mi. S of Mt. Orab	Yes	E
C	Griggs Reservoir	385	US 33, 7 mi. S of Dublin (Scioto River)	Yes	U
NE	Guilford Lake State Park	396	SR 172, 4 mi. NW of Lisbon (Beaver Creek)	Yes	10
C	Hargus Lake (at A.W. Marion State Park)	146	2 mi. NE of Circleville off US 22 or SR 188	Yes	E
NW	Harrison Lake State Park	96	5 mi. SW of Fayette, off US 20	Yes	E
NE	Highlandown Lake Wildlife Area	170	NW of Highlandtown f of SR 39	Yes	E
C	Hoover Reservoir	3,300	NE of Columbus, 4 mi. E of Westerville	Yes	6
C	Indian Lake State Park	5,800	Off US 33, 12 mi. NW of Bellefontaine	Yes	U
SE	Jackson City Reservoir (Hammertown Lake)	190	On SR 776, S of Jackson	Yes	E
SE	Jackson Lake	243	On SR 279, 2 mi. W of Oak Hill	Yes	10
C	Kiser Lake State Park	380	SR 235, 2 mi. S of Quincy	Yes	No
C	Knox Lake Wildlife Area	495	SR 95, 1 mi. NE of Fredericktown (E Br. Kokosing River)	Yes	10
C	Kokosing Lake Wldlf. Area	154	3 mi. NW of Fredericktown, CR 6	Yes	10
SE	Lake Alma State Park	64	SR 349, 1 mi. NE of Wellston	Yes	E
SE	Lake Hope State Park	127	4 mi. N. of Zaleski	Yes	E
NW	Lake LaComte	128	1½ mi. SW of Fostoria	No	10
SE	Lake Logan State Park	400	2 mi. SW of Logan on SR 664	Yes	10
SW	Lake Loramie	825	1 mi. S of Minster, off SR 66	Yes	U
NE	Lake Medina	100	2 mi. NE of Medina, on SR 18	No	No
NE	Lake Milton	1,685	SR 534 at Co. Rd. 18, 15 mi. W of Youngstown	Yes	U
SE	Lake White State Park	337	4 mi. SW of Waverly, SR 101	Yes	U
NE	Leesville Lake Wildlife Area – MWCD	1,000	2 mi. SE of Sharrodsville off SR 212	Yes	10
NW	Lima Lake	85	3 mi. E of Lima, SR 81	No	No

Section of state	Lake	Acreage	Location	Ramp	Max. HP
NW	Lost Creek Reservoir	121	1 mi. E of Lima, High St. Rd.	No	E
C	Madison Lake State Park	100	SR 665, 4 mi. E. of London	Yes	E
NW	Metzger Lake	160	1½ mi. E of Lima, High St. Rd.	No	E
NW	Metzger Marsh Wildlife Area	528	Off SR 2, 1 mi. E of Bono (Lake Erie & Ward Canal)	Yes	U
NE	Mill Creek Park	105	City of Youngstown	Yes	4
NE	Mogadore Reservoir	1,000	SR 43, 6 mi. S of Kent (Hunting with city permit)	Yes	E
SE	Monroe Lake Wildlife Area	43	5 mi. N of Woodsfield, SR 8	Yes	E
NE	Mosquito Creek Lake	7,850	SR 88 at Mecca & SR 46	Yes	U
NW	Nettle Lake (fee required)	94	4 mi. NE of Cooney, off SR 49	Yes	U
SE	New Lexington Reservoir	27	2 mi. N of New Lexington, off SR 13	No	E
NW	New London Reservoir	213	2 mi. SW of N. London on Town Ln. Rd.	Yes	E
NE	Nimisila Reservoir	811	2 mi. S of SR 619 on S. Main St.	Yes	E
SE	Ohio Power Recreation Area (Ponds)	2,000	9 mi. NE of McConnelsville on SR 76	No	E
C	O'Shaughnessy Reservoir	920	SR 257, 3 mi. N of Dublin	Yes	U
NW	Oxbow Lake Wildlife Area	45	8 mi. NW of Defiance on SR 15	Yes	E
SE	Paint Creek State Lake	1,190	US 50, 17 mi. E of Hillsboro	Yes	U
NE	Piedmont Lake — MWCD	2,310	US 22, 1 mi. NE of Smyrna	Yes	10
SE	Pike Lake State Park & Forest	13	5 mi. NW of Morgantown off SR 124	Yes	E
NE	Pleasant Hill Lake — MWCD	850	SR 95, 4 mi. W of Perrysville (Clear Fork Br., Mohican River)	Yes	U
NE	Portage Lakes State Park	1,651	SR 93, 4 mi. S of Akron (Hunting — Long Lake only)	Yes	U
NE	Punderson Lake	101	4 mi. N of US 422 on SR 44	Yes	E
NE	Pymatuning State Park	14,650	SR 85, 2 mi. E of Andover	Yes	10
NE	Resthaven Wildlife Area	322	SR 269, Castalia	Yes	E
SW	Rocky Fork State Park	2,080	SR 124, 6 mi. SE of Hillsboro	Yes	U
SE	Rose Lake	17	2 mi. S of Old Man's Cave on SR 374	No	E
SE	Ross Lake Wildlife Area	140	3½ mi. E of Chillicothe on Hydell Rd.	Yes	E
SW	Rush Run Wildlife Area	58	4 mi. SE of Camden on Co. Rd. Northern	Yes	E
SE	Salt Fork Lake	2,952	8 mi. NE of Cambridge off SR 21 (Salt Fork Creek)	Yes	U
SE	Senecaville Lake — MWCD	3,550	1 mi. E of Senecaville off SR 313	Yes	180
SE	Shawnee State Forest	75	On SR 125, NW of Friendship 2 lakes, 5 ponds)	Yes	E
NE	Shreve Lake Wildlife Area	58	1 mi. W of Shreve	Yes	E
SE	Snowden Lake	131	Off US 50, ½ mi. NE of Albany	Yes	6
NE	Spencer Lake Wildlife Area	70	2 mi. E of Spencer off SR 162 (Black River)	Yes	E

Section of state	Lake	Acreage	Location	Ramp	Max. HP
SW	Spring Valley Wildlife Area	90	2 mi. S of Spring Valley, E of US 42 (Little Miami River)	No	E
NE	Springfield Lake	268	S of US 224 at Lakemore	Yes	U
SW	Stonelick State Park	171	At Edenton on SR 727 and SR 133	Yes	E
SE	Strouds Run State Park (Dow Lake)	160	SR 50, 5 mi. E. of Athens	Yes	10
NE	Tappan Lake — MWCD	2,350	US 250 at Tappan	Yes	120
SW	Taylorsville Dam	8	On SR 440, 2 mi. E of Vandalia (Great Miami River)	No	E
SE	Tycoon Lake Wildlife Area	204	On SR 554 NE of Rio Grande	Yes	E
NW	Van Buren State Park	53	Off US 25, SE of Van Buren	Yes	E
SE	Vesuvius Lake	105	9 mi. N of of Ironton, E of SR 93	Yes	E
SE	Veto Lake Wildlife Area	160	On SR 339, 8 mi. NW of Belpre	Yes	10
NE	Wellington Reservoir	160	W ½ mi. off SR 58 on Jones Rd.	Yes	E
SE	Wellston Wildlife Area (Lake Rupert)	325	4 mi. S of McArthur on SR 93	Yes	10
NE	West Branch State Park (M.J. Kirwan Res.)	2,650	5 mi. E of Ravenna on SR 5 (Mahoning River)	Yes	U
NE	Willard Reservoir	285	2 mi. E of Willard on SR 61	Yes	E
NE	Wills Creek Lake — MWCD	900	SR 83 at Marquand Mills	Yes	10
SE	Wolf Run State Park	220	Off SR 21 at Belle Valley	Yes	10
NE	Zepernick Lake Wildlife Area	41	On SR 172, 2 mi. E of New Alexander	Yes	E

Cameron Tenhover battles a hybrid striped bass at East Fork Lake, 20 miles east of Cincinnati.

Ohio River anglers fish for sauger at Meldahl Dam east of Cincinnati.

Ohio River Sauger

By Jim Morris

Mike Dirr doesn't fish the wall on the weekends.

"It gets too crazy," he said.

Dirr will fish the wall during the week. It's still busy, but there's usually room to catch fish.

The wall leads to the locks at the Meldahl Dam, on the Ohio River about 30 miles east of Cincinnati.

The attraction is sauger and plenty of them.

It's not an uncommon sight to see boats lined up, two deep in some places, along the wall in the cold of winter. Anglers will be bundled in the warmest clothing they can find, just as long as they can operate their fishing gear and get a line to the bottom to catch sauger.

Five degrees. Zero. It doesn't deter the true sauger fisherman.

The areas below the dams and in the creek mouths are prime spots for finding sauger when it gets cold on the Ohio River. They stay and bite through early spring, attracting hearty anglers from Ohio, Kentucky, Indiana and sometimes farther away.

"It gets so bad here on the weekends that there just isn't enough room for everyone," said Dirr, who lives in nearby Batavia. "I've seen guys get into fistfights over a spot on the wall. It reminds me of the Maumee River during the walleye runs."

He said there will typically be 25-30 boats in that small spot on weekends, and usually 8-12 on weekdays. There aren't many tie-ups on the wall, so anglers often use industrial magnets to keep their boats on the steel structure. "They're so strong, you can't pull them straight out. You kind of have to pry them off," said Grenvil Roberts of Xenia, who was fishing there with Roy Edwards, also of Xenia.

Sometimes it's important to be able to grab that magnet and get off the wall quickly.

That's when the whistle blows and a large barge is headed through the locks. The fishing boats have to scatter in a hurry to get out of the barge's way. But once it's all-clear, those boats jump right back on the wall as if those magnets were pulling them.

Roberts and Edwards don't mind the cold, because they know that it is the best time to catch sauger and there's not much they can do about it.

"When it's cold, you just have to wear a lot of clothes," Roberts said. "Sometimes I look like I weigh 400 pounds, I have on so many layers of clothes. But that doesn't matter. I come down here three or four times a week."

"It's a fun fishery to me," said Mark Hicks of Athens, who wrote the book *Fishing the Ohio River*. "On just about any day a couple of guys can go out and catch 60 fish or so and have plenty of action," Hicks said.

The creel limit is 10 per person, so many cull smaller saugers to take home a bag of 16-22-inch fish. Most saugers weigh less than three pounds.

A popular way to fish for them is to use a jigging spoon tipped with a minnow. You can also use a vibrating bait, such as a Silver Buddy or Bullet Bait, bounced on the bottom.

Most anglers fish straight down and find the sauger has a light bite like its cousin the walleye, usually hitting as you pick up the bait from the bottom.

Hicks said sauger fishermen usually don't catch many other species of fish in winter, because they fish on the bottom in fairly deep water, about 20 feet. Crappies, hybrid striped bass and white bass also bite on the Ohio River in winter, they're usually found at shallower depths.

ODNR photo

A winter angler who knows the Ohio River has a good chance of taking a daily limit of 10 saugers.

Harold Barefoot, foreground, with fishing buddies Joe Walsh (standing) and Bob Roth enjoy a day on Stillwater River.

Southwest Ohio Rivers
The Great Miami, Little Miami, Mad and Stillwater

By Jim Morris

Three rivers flow into Dayton with some of the best fishing found north of the city.

The Great Miami: You name it and there's a possibility you might catch it in the Great Miami. With vastly improved water quality in recent years, a wide variety of fish can be found in this river that runs from above Indian Lake all the way to the Ohio River.

Above Dayton, at stops in towns like Sidney, Piqua, Troy and Tipp City you are likely to find super fishing for bass, especially smallmouth. You can fish from a canoe at different times in the year, but most prefer bank fishing or wading.

There are loads of panfish, catfish and a growing number of northern pike. The state stocks 150,000 saugeyes each year and fishing seems to be hot for them usually below the many low-head dams. The dams south of Dayton are also hot spots for saugeye fishing. A "do not eat" health advisory remains in effect south of Dayton for bottom feeders.

The Little Miami: The first thing that will strike you is the beauty of the river. It's a national and state scenic river and deserves those distinctions all the way from Clark County to the Ohio River.

Depending on the water levels, most of the river is prime canoe territory and a good place for bass fishing. There are plenty of smallmouth and rock bass. Most other species can be caught in the river, including a few muskies down stream from Cowan Lake. It's a good river for channel cats.

Try to avoid weekend fishing during good weather and leave the Little Miami to the canoeists, because there are plenty of them. Many liveries make it one of the best canoeing rivers in Ohio.

The Mad River: The Mad isn't all that swift, especially in the northern portion. Like any river, it can get high and swift at certain times of the year, but generally it's a peaceful river in most places.

It's also like two rivers in one. The northern part of the Mad, and its tributaries around Bellefontaine, is perhaps Ohio's best trout river. The Division of Wildlife stocks brown trout there each year and they can be caught from spring through fall in the pools. Fly fishermen have adopted the Mad.

The southern part of the Mad, below Springfield, is a good fishery for small-mouth bass, rock bass and other species. After Buck Creek joins the flow, the water is generally too warm to support trout. However, a long-standing state record for smallmouth came out of the lower Mad, topped a few years ago by a Lake Erie smallmouth.

The Stillwater: Like the Mad, the Stillwater doesn't always live up to its name. Depending on the time of year, some swift-moving water can be found on this very clean, well-cared-for state scenic river.

There's a debate in the region as to whether the smallmouth bass fishing is better on the Stillwater or the Great Miami. It doesn't really matter, since it can be outstanding in both places. Largemouth are also found on the Stillwater, which also supports a large population of crappies, bluegills and catfish.

Jim Morris photo

Joe Dickerson, Cincinnati, fishes for brown trout at the Mad River.

19

Spring fishing is golden when James Cantor (left) and brother, Joey, of Athens, attend trout derby at Dow Lake.

Trout in Ohio

By Jim Robey

Trout fishing in Ohio requires knowing where to go, getting to the good spots at the right time and employing the proper angling technique. An angler who can put these things together can be successful in this state.

Ohio presents three main trout fishing opportunities. They are:

• Fishing for keeper-size golden and rainbow trout stocked in March and April, mainly in southeast Ohio.

• Stream fishing for river browns at the Mad River in western Ohio and the Clear Fork of the Mohican River south of Mansfield.

• Steelhead fishing during the winter and spring at four rivers that flow into Lake Erie in northeast Ohio.

Trout Fishing at Southeast Ohio Lakes

More than 38,000 keeper-size trout are stocked at Ohio lakes in March and April. Most are placed at reservoirs in the southeast section of the state.

Anglers who like to catch trout won't have a better opportunity than when the "catchables" are released. Most of the fish weigh a half pound or more and are rainbows or golden trout, a color phase of the rainbow.

Spring trout action peaks at the southeast Ohio lakes with three trout fishing derbies that draw anglers of all ages. And regardless of the age, everybody seems to have an enjoyable outing.

The location and time of each trout fishing festival, and the approximate number of fish stocked:

Stroud's Run State Park (Dow Lake), 160 acres, near Athens, second Saturday of April, about 4,000 trout.
Jackson City Reservoir (Hammertown Lake) at Jackson, 190 acres, third Saturday of April, about 4,000 trout.
Turkey Creek Lake, in Shawnee State

Park near Portsmouth, 75 acres, fourth Saturday of April, about 2,500 trout.

Although these have been the traditional trout festival dates, it would be advisable to call the district wildlife office before the middle of March to confirm that times have not been changed. Call 614-594-2211.

While double checking the trout derbies, ask for dates of other trout reservoirs stocked at southeast Ohio in March and April. A number of them are stocked in March.

Other reservoirs that receive trout are:

Belmont Lake, Barkcamp State Park, 117 acres of water, one mile east of Belmont.
Wolf Run Lake in Wolf Run State Park, 220 acres, off Ohio 21 at Belle Valley.
Rose Lake, 17 acres, walk-in lake near Old Man's Cave in Hocking Hills State Park.
New Lexington City Reservoir, 27 acres, two miles north of New Lexington off Ohio 13.
Monroe Lake, in Monroe Lake Wildlife Area, 40 acres, on Ohio 800, five miles north of Woodsfield.
Forked Run Lake, in Forked Run State Park, 104 acres, off Ohio 124 near Reedsville.

Other lakes that receive a stocking of keeper-size rainbows or goldens in the spring include **Lake Antrim,** a city park reservoir on the north side of Columbus, and **Punderson Lake,** in Punderson State Park, east of Cleveland at Newbury and Lock No. 4 on the Ohio Canal in Starke County.

Many people like to start fishing within minutes after the trout have been delivered by the Fish Ohio trucks. Usually it takes a few hours before trout are ready to hit, if not a day or so. Good fishing may continue for a few weeks after the stocking, if not for a couple of months or longer.

Lures that take trout include the Rooster Tail, Mepps spinner, Panther Martin and small crankbaits. Other trout baits include Berkley's trout formula, cheese, corn, miniature marshmallows and live worms.

The trout creel limit at inland lakes is five.

It's trout-stocking time when boat ramps are this crowded in late winter at about 10 southeast Ohio lakes.

Trout in Mad River and Clear Fork

The upper reaches of the Mad River in Champaign and Logan counties and the Clear Fork of the Mohican River south of Mansfield are two streams where 10,000 advanced fingerling brown trout are stocked each year, at each location.

At the time of stocking in the fall the browns are about 7 to 8 inches. The fish can attain a length of 10 inches by the following spring, according to biologists.

In addition to the fingerlings, from 10,000 to 40,000 browns from 3 to 4 inches may be stocked in May, if the trout hatcheries have a surplus of fish. The minimum size limit for keeping a trout at either stream is 10 inches.

"I'd say our trout program is based mainly on the stocking of the advanced fingerlings because we have a better survival with them," explains Steve Graham, fish management supervisor in central Ohio.

Serious trout anglers like the policy of stocking fingerlings, as opposed to the release of "catchables," fish large enough to keep before they are stocked.

The anglers feel the Mad River and Clear Fork are producing a more natural fishery under the fingerling program. Surveys taken at the rivers show that many anglers have adopted the practice of catch-and-release fishing as their own contribution toward enhancing Ohio trout fishing.

Mad River has been stocked with browns during the 1990s. Some of the old, surviving browns weigh from five to 10 pounds. One brown weighing 12 pounds has been caught and released, according to fishing reports.

Either these older trout are doing a fantastic job of eluding anglers, or catch-and-release participants are achieving excellent results with their conservation efforts.

Trout fishing on the Mad River is along some 30 miles of spring-fed water upstream from the Clark-Champaign County Line, and includes several tributaries. One of them, Mac-O-Chee Creek, has been given special designation.

On Mac-O-Chee Creek, fishing is limited to "artificial lure or fly having a single barbless hook. The bag limit is one and the minimum size limit on the Mad River and tributaries is 10 inches. Five is the normal creel limit for trout at inland waters.

The Clear Fork of the Mohican also has a section for artificial lure or fly having a single barbless hook. It is the area from "the State Route 13 Bridge in Belleville to the State Route 95 Bridge in Butler." Trout are taken in the Clear Fork of the Mohican down to Pleasant Hill Lake, and sometimes in the lake.

Fly fishing has become so popular that about 50 percent of the brown trout anglers fish with fly rod. Many do very well and fish year around.

Despite the success of the fly fishers, they cannot catch as many trout as anglers using other methods, according to a state survey in 1994.

The study found that anglers using artificial lures caught .69 trout per hour on the Mad River, compared to .59 per hour for those using live bait and .38 percent per hour for those fishing with a fly.

Brown Trout

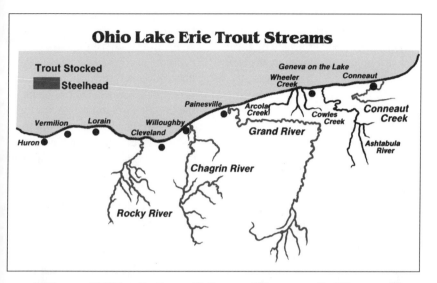

Ohio Lake Erie Trout Streams

Trout Stocked
Steelhead

Geneva on the Lake · Wheeler Creek · Conneaut · Painesville · Arcola Creek · Cowles Creek · Conneaut Creek · Grand River · Vermilion · Lorain · Willoughby · Cleveland · Huron · Ashtabula River · Chagrin River · Rocky River

The Mighty Steelhead Trout

By Jim Robey

Steelhead, a rainbow trout that migrates into big water and comes back as a big fish, is doing better than ever at four streams in northern Ohio.

"The reason is the wild Little Manistee strain of steelhead we've been stocking," explains Phil Hillman, district fish management supervisor in northeast Ohio.

"We are stocking 50,000 Little Manistee steelhead in the Rocky River, Chagrin River, Grand River and Conneaut Creek, for a total of 200,000 per year," Hillman said.

While the numbers roughly are the same as the strain of rainbow-steelhead produced in the Ohio Fish Hatchery at London, it's the only thing that hasn't changed.

Since going to the wild strain of steelhead obtained from Michigan, steelhead fishing has escalated to a level far beyond what it was five years ago.

"For every Manistee steelhead we stock it would take up to three to five London hatchery strain fish to produce as much fishing," Hillman said.

The biologist believes the Little Manistee is a superior wild strain of steelhead because it's produced under low light conditions and with little human contact. The fish is made available to Ohio in trade for channel catfish.

Brian Flechsig, Columbus, with 9-pound steelhead taken on fly at Conneaut Creek.

In mid-April, when the trout are 6 to 9 inches, they are set free in the four rivers. The trout are protected by a state law that prohibits taking more than two trout or salmon from Sept. 1 through April 30, plus a 12-inch minimum size limit that applies all year at Lake Erie and its tributaries.

The fish migrate into Lake Erie in May where the growth rate increases dramatically. After the first summer, a Little Manistee steelhead may be 18 inches long, 25 inches after two summers and 29 inches after three.

London strain steelhead grew to 14 inches the first summer, 22 inches the second and 25 inches the third.

Besides a faster growing strain of steelhead, we have better fishing through fall and winter, plus a longer period to fish in the spring, Hillman says.

"These steelhead have provided some fabulous fishing," he added.

Steelhead from 7 to 12 pounds, perhaps larger, will provide fall to spring fishing in the Rocky River, Chagrin River, Grand River and Conneaut Creek through the 1990s, and beyond. Steelhead also will be taken from piers, points along Lake Erie and from the lake itself during the summer and early fall.

Steelhead releases in Ohio date back to 1969, but the program was greatly expanded in 1986, about the time coho salmon returns were declared unsatisfactory and phased out. Unlike salmon, steelhead do not die when they return to their home rivers.

The steelhead generally return to their home streams around the middle of October and remain in the rivers through April. Water temperature in the fall of about 50 degrees, along with increase river flow, prompts the steel-

head to move into the rivers from the lake.

Hillman says steelhead can be found in deeper pools along 18 miles of the Rocky River in Cuyahoga County from Ohio 480 downstream to the mouth; at the Chagrin River in Lake County for six miles from Ohio 84 to the mouth; in some 32 miles of the Grand River in Lake and Ashtabula counties from Ohio 534 to the mouth; and in approximately 20 miles of Conneaut Creek in Ashtabula county from the Pennsylvania line to the mouth of the stream.

Steelhead tackle used by Hillman consists of an 8 1/2-to 13-foot rod and a spinning reel spooled with clear, 6-pound monofilament line. "The fish are easily spooked," Hillman said.

When fishing at beaches, the outlets of creeks or from piers such as the one at Geneva State Park, Hillman suggests spinners such as the Roostertail or Blue Fox, K-O Wobblers or Little Cleos.

For bait fishing at the rivers, it's hard to beat a bag of salmon eggs about the size of a thumbnail with just enough splitshot on the line to cause the bait to bounce slowly along the bottom.

Another trick is to put on a 1/16 or 1/34 ounce jig, depending on river flow, cut the tail off the grub and load the hook with live maggots. It sounds repulsive, but it works. Bobber rigs frequently are used to help keep the bait from snagging on the bottom.

During the winter, fish may be found where the current glides into the deeper pools. Riffles can be productive in early spring.

A number of anglers have fished for steelhead with fly fishing tackle and some have been successful..

GEORGE V. VOINOVICH
GOVERNOR

STATE OF OHIO
OFFICE OF THE GOVERNOR
COLUMBUS 43266-0601

As an avid angler, I am always proud to promote an outdoor recreation that thousands of Ohioans and out-of-state visitors enjoy. Fishing is a wonderful, inexpensive, family-oriented activity that adds so much to the quality of life we enjoy here in Ohio.

Whether you're out for bluegill, walleye, trout, catfish or bass, Ohio offers some of the best fishing opportunities in the world. Our rivers, lakes and streams provide anglers with an endless variety of exciting challenges.

There's only one more thing to be said about our great Ohio fishing: Get out and enjoy it!

Good fishing!

George V. Voinovich
        Governor

Bill Reinke photo.

Steven Stevens (left) and Bruce John, both from Toledo, take advantage of the spring walleye run in Maumee River.

River Walleyes Depend on Weather

By Jim Robey

Spring fishing for the run of walleyes in the Maumee and Sandusky rivers looks promising for the next few years, but only if anglers get a break with the weather.

A good population of walleyes is available from the hatch of 1991, '93 and '94. These walleyes range from 16 to 24 inches and large numbers of them will make their way up the rivers to spawn.

The survivors from the super hatch of walleyes in 1986 will include females weighing from 10 to 15 pounds. Anglers can look forward to catching them, too.

Walleyes hatched in 1996, a good

year for spawning, will contribute heavily to the fishing in 1998, '99 and into the 2000s, as will walleyes hatched in other years.

Still, keeping the spring run in perspective, river conditions will play the major role in determining angling success. Few types of fishing are so dependent on weather.

"You must have a good river flow - not too high and not too low," says Larry Goedde, district fish management supervisor in northwest Ohio.

Through the mid 1990s, spring weather did not favor the Ohio angler. Unusually cool temperatures and exces-

26

sive rainfall was a major setback for spring walleye fishing.

The law of averages says this can't continue. Optimists have to believe that the coming springs will be more normal, with slowly rising water temperature, a modest amount of rainfall and happy days for fishing.

Most springs, after a couple days of sunshine, many anglers are anxious to put on a pair of boots, wade into the Maumee or Sandusky River and cast a jig-head with twister into the walleye water. The arrival at the streams often precedes the actual run of fish by two or three weeks.

What you want to follow closely is the water temperature. When it gets up to 44 degrees, or higher, walleye fishing time has arrived.

That's when walleyes on their spawning run swim up river from Lake Erie, including those heavyweight females that weigh 10 pounds or more.

The Division of Wildlife usually advises anglers they can expect the peak of the walleye run to occur around the second week of April. Some years the fishing is outstanding the third and fourth weeks of March, depending on water temperature and river flow.

During the last week of March a few years ago, Cliff and John Cook of Grove City were seen as they came ashore from the Maumee River at Schroeder Farm's Campground, Perrysburg, with one of the greatest catches of walleyes anyone had ever seen.

The brothers had caught 10 walleyes that weighed 90 pounds. They could barely lift their stringer.

Bruce John of Toledo, who fishes the Maumee River in the spring, had a great day on the Maumee, as you can see from the expression on his face. His picture is on the cover of this guide.

The annual run of walleyes often continues through April. It attracts thousands of anglers from all parts of Ohio, plus many out-of-state fishermen.

Besides water temperature, walleyes are stimulated to move up rivers by an increase in river flow, although excessive flow can make fishing impossible, if not unsafe.

The best place to fish for walleyes in the Maumee River is from the Ohio Turnpike Bridge downstream to the I-475 Bridge at Maumee and Perrysburg. About 90 percent of the walleyes caught in the Maumee are taken from this area.

At the Sandusky River, the prime fishing is at the City of Fremont from Brady's Island to Roger Young Park.

Most fishing is done by wading or casting from shore. Cartop boats can be used on both rivers. The better sections for trailered boats is limited to the lower portions of both rivers where the water is deeper.

Bill Reinke photo.

Jig and twister combo takes most of the river-run walleyes caught in the Maumee and Sandusky rivers.

MAUMEE RIVER

90% of the walleyes taken from the Maumee River come from the Maumee-Perrysburg section shown on this map. This also is a top area for white bass.

Fishing Spots
marked by Darrell Allison,
District 2 fish management supervisor

1. Harrison St. parking
2. Side Cut Park. Parking and carry-on boat launch
3. Side Cut Park extension. Parking and carry-on boat launch
4. Fort Miami Launching access
5. Maple St. launching
6. Orleans Park. Parking and launching ramp
7. Fort Meigs (lower lot) parking and carry-on boat launch
8. Fort Meigs (upper lot) parking only
9. Hull Prairie Rd. parking
10. Divine Word Seminary parking

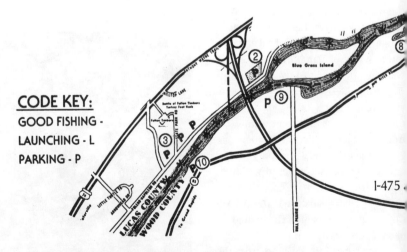

CODE KEY:
GOOD FISHING -
LAUNCHING - L
PARKING - P

NO PARKING ALONG HWY 65 AND OTHER RESTRICTED AREAS
NO OVERNIGHT CAMPING . NO LITTERING

SANDUSKY

OHIO TURNPIKE

④ P/L

⑤ P/L

PERRYSBURG

I-75

M/R

R/G

M

L

M

M

M/R

Fish with Caution

Whether wading, or in a boat, caution is required. High water and cold water is a dangerous combination. River conditions must be respected.

Nearly all walleyes are caught on doll flies or weighted jigs with twister tails. Colors used are white, yellow, green, chartreuse, red, pink, smoke or something else. You are never sure what color the walleyes will respond to from one day to the next, so have a selection.

Remember these are spawning walleyes and that means the fish are not aggressive feeders. Patience is a necessity.

Special Regulations

Do not be tempted to try snagging. It's strictly illegal. The person fishing next to you could be a wildlife officer. During the spawning run, some officers dress as anglers and patrol the river with a fishing rod in one hand and a citation book in their pocket.

Special regulations that must be observed from March 1 to May 1 include no night fishing, no more than one single hook on a line and the hook must be 1/2-inch or smaller from point to shank. Treble hooks are not allowed before May 1.

These regulations are outlined in the Ohio Digest of Fishing Regulations that is distributed where fishing licenses are sold. Also described in detail is the area where the special regulations apply.

The walleye run in the Maumee and Sandusky rivers will be followed by a run of white bass that will peak around the middle of May. White bass numbers have declined in recent years, but an improvement was noted in 1996. The positive trend in white bass reproduction is expected to be reflected with better fishing in 1997 and '98.

Call for Updated Reports

Current information about river conditions, water temperature and the fishing outlook can be obtained by calling 1-800-BUCKEYE after March 1.

For the Maumee River you can call the Walleye Hotline at (419) 893-9740.

Drive-up bait and tackle shops along Maumee River offer wide assortment of jigs, plastic twisters and landing nets.

Lake Erie....Fishing Forecast

By Jim Robey

So you've been looking for a place to stay along Lake Erie. You saw the boat you've always wanted, the price is right, but...

Go for it.

Lake Erie is not going away. It's one thing we can count on as we finish out the millennium .

If it's the fishing that concerns you, relax. Good years lie ahead. In fact, they'll be much better for perch.

Moreover, people still will be calling Lake Erie the "walleye capital of the world," if not the "walleye and small-mouth bass capital."

In five of the last seven years, the walleye hatch has been better than aver-age, each time lifting the population of the fish in Lake Erie by about 20 to 25 million.

The two years of unsatisfactory hatches were recorded in 1992 and '95. Walleye numbers dropped 20 to 25 mil-lion on each of these years.

Roger Knight, supervisor of the Lake Erie Fish Research Unit at Sandusky, said he was pleased with the walleye hatch in 1996.

Walleye fishing in 1997 is expected to be down a little from 1996 because of the low hatch in '95. But while the numbers of fish may be off a little, the size of the fish will be better, Knight says.

Come 1998, 1999 and 2000, when the '96 hatched walleyes are two, three and four years old, respectively, anglers can anticipate excellent fishing for fish from the '96 class, as well as walleyes from other year classes.

Some walleyes in Lake Erie have sur

Jim Lowe, Dayton, would rather be fishing Lake Erie.

vived a number of years and attained an age of 10 years or more. Knight believes the lake has some walleyes that weigh up to 17 pounds, or more. The person who catches one will be able to claim a state fish record.

The current record for walleye is a Lake Erie fish that weighed 15.95 pounds when taken on March 24, 1995 by Mike Beldel of Fayetteville, Pa.

Yellow perch, one of the big concerns at Lake Erie, is making a strong come-back. Good hatches of perch were noted in 1993 and '94, followed by a less suc-cessful spawn in 1995.

The 1996 perch hatch was excellent. Fishing for the popular species in the fall of '96 was encouraging. Many were able to take a limit of perch (30 per person) within a couple of hours.

Adding to Lake Erie more than ever is the smallmouth bass. "We don't attempt to measure the population of small-mouth, but we know from all the fishing reports we receive that smallmouth pop-ulation is increasing," Knight said

Lake Erie Charter Captains on the Web

By Jim Robey

Finding a boat captain at Lake Erie who will take you fishing when you want to go is easier since the Lake Erie Charter Boat Association (LECBA) has gone on the World Wide Web.

If you are one of the millions of on-line personal computer users, you can visit the charter captains' home page on the internet and obtain Lake Erie fishing information at - www.dcache.net/lecba

LECBA is the oldest and largest group of charter captains with 375 members, including supporting businesses and associate members. Every captain is listed on the LECBA web page, by name, home marina and name-of boat.

With such a detailed list of captains serving anglers, it should be easy to locate one that will serve your fishing interest, whether it's going for walleyes, smallmouth bass or perch fishing in the fall.

Bob Collins, president of the LECBA, says that anglers who do not have computer access to the web, can get infor-mation from his group by calling 1-800-LECBA10, or by writing: LECBA, 4905 E. Court Drive, Port Clinton, OH 43452.

Twenty-five years ago, there were fewer than 35 licensed charter boat skippers on the lake, but the number has risen to more than 1,000. A number are part timers who don't belong to an association, but have been licensed by the Coast Guard to operate a charter boat.

Charter boat rates range from $350 to $450 for up to six passengers fishing for seven to eight hours, depending mainly on services provided.

That's a healthy hunk of cash, so don't be bashful about asking what's included.

For example, does the fee include bait, tackle and ice? Usually, it does not include tackle, nor does it include bait when soft craws are purchased for smallmouth bass fishing.

If the charter is for a full day and

Continued on page 157

John Combs shows bragging-size walleye to his brother, Howard.

The long pier at Metzger Wildlife Area presents excellent access for Lake Erie bank fishermen.

Bank on Lake Erie

By Jim Robey

Anyone who has booked charter boat fishing trips at Lake Erie probably has had some disappointing days when it was too rough to venture on the big lake.

Even when you call the night before to confirm your reservation and check on weather, conditions can change overnight and force canceling the trip.

An alternative to coming home empty handed is fishing from one of the piers, points, along riprap banks or from the docks where permitted. Some excellent catches of fish can be made from these places.

Moreover, you are likely to meet anglers who wouldn't fish from a boat if you offered them a free trip. Many people don't care for those rockin' and rollin' seas.

These anglers want to plant their feet on solid ground, or cement in the case of the piers. Some of them want to set up a lawn chair, bait up and throw in two lines, sit back and relax.

The relaxing may be cut short because a variety of fish hang around docks and piers, including crappies, perch, catfish, sheepshead, smallmouth bass, rock bass and carp. Even steelhead trout and salmon are possible from piers east of Cleveland.

Here's some of the special places you can bank on at Lake Erie:

A. Metzgar Marsh Wildlife Area - This long pier protruding into Lake Erie is located west of Port Clinton by Crane Creek State Park. It's heavily utilized on weekends, but you'll find plenty of room to fish. Perch is the favorite species taken by pier fishermen, followed by sheepshead, catfish and sometimes walleye. A two-lane boat ramp serves boat owners.

B. Portage River Access - This access, two miles west of Port Clinton on Ohio 2, provides shore fishing on the Portage River. A two-lane boat ramp affords convenient access to the river and to Lake Erie. Fishing is for perch, walleye, white bass, smallmouth bass and catfish.

C. Catawba Island State Park - This park lies on the northwest side of Catawba Island, just east of Port Clinton. It has a fishing pier that is roughly T-shaped, with ample parking nearby, plus picnic tables and restroom facilities to go along with the good perch fishing. It's also a fine smallmouth and rock bass spot in spring. Fishermen do well here on both species. A four-lane ramp serves boat owners.

D. Mazurik Access - Mazurik, off Ohio 163 on North Shore Blvd., not far from Catawba Island State Park, opened in 1989 and added a badly needed four-lane boat launching ramp, plus parking for 170 cars and trailers and an excellent place for pier fishing. The pier that is accessible to the handicapped has five fishing platforms and offers anglers a chance to catch walleye, perch, white bass, channel catfish and smallmouth bass.

E. Dempsey Access - An excellent pier south of Marblehead with a four-lane boat ramp, Dempsey offers fishing, restrooms and parking facilities. Dempsey is a popular place with Lake Erie fishermen because perch can be caught, plus channel catfish and other bottom feeders. The pier lies just south of Marblehead.

F. Old Bay Bridge - This bridge just west of Sandusky is no longer traveled since it was replaced by a new, four-lane highway across Sandusky Bay, but anglers are getting a lot of use from the old structure. Anglers who drive onto the bridge from the west side, find lots of parking and plenty of fishing. This is a prime catfish spot that offers some smallmouth fishing in spring and fall months. Perch tend to run small, but there are plenty of them.

G. Battery Park - Battery Park in downtown Sandusky isn't a pier, as such; rather, it's a cluster of mini-piers and bits of water front where fishermen gather to try for crappie, smallmouth, perch, and catfish. Some segments are private, so make sure you drop your lines in places where fishing is allowed.

H. Huron Pier - This fishing access on the waterfront in downtown Huron consists of a long pier that terminates at a lighthouse where the Huron River flows into Lake Erie. A popular place in early spring through fall, anglers have a good chance of catching perch, smallmouth bass, crappie and catfish. As at a number of other piers, it often holds true that you catch more when you fish farther out on a pier, but that's not always the case.

I. Lorain Municipal Park - This is an inviting small pier, more or less in the downtown area. It offers excellent perch fishing in early spring and late fall, and fair action on perch, catfish and sheepshead throughout the summer.

J. Rocky River and Cleveland - Rocky River has a small pier that offers fair fishing for perch, catfish and the ever-present Lake Erie sheepshead. Cleveland has three very well known spots: Edgewater Park, the East Ninth Street Pier and the East 72nd Street Pier. They all get heavy use and produce good mixed fishing in all seasons, but when winds are high, waves seem to break over them a bit more than at protected areas.

K. Grand River - At the mouth of the Grand River a fishing pier beckons anglers while nearby Headlands State Park has a breakwall suitable for fishing. These spots offer some action on steelhead trout fishing in the fall inasmuch as the Grand is one of Ohio's steelhead streams. In the spring, expect fair fishing for larger than average perch, plus the occasional smallmouth and various bottom fish.

L. Geneva State Park - The $13 million marina with a six-lane boat ramp and 383 boat slips, dedicated on Oct. 18, 1988, is a great addition for Lake Erie bank anglers as well as those who fish from a boat. An entrance channel connecting the harbor with the lake is 100 feet wide and 800 feet long. It is lined with breakwater structures providing a fishing access to Lake Erie. The breakwater on the east side has a concrete walkway and hand railing. Anglers fishing from the breakwaters may catch perch, catfish, sheepshead and other species. There also is the possibility of casting into the lake and taking steelhead stocked in Ohio, or hooking a salmon that has moved in from Pennsylvania or New York.

M. Geneva-On-The-Lake - The lake front just north of Geneva has a small pier that's utilized for much the same species as the Grand River pier. Anglers seeking trout and salmon here favor bottom fishing spawn bags, maggots on ice spoons, and various shiny spoons and brightly colored crankbaits. Action can be very good in late fall. Perch, sheepshead and catfish are caught from this location.

N. Ashtabula - Ashtabula has a city park breakwater that's fishable, and the Conneaut City Park has another. Parking is a bit limited at Conneaut, but fishing can be good at both places. Perch are the main species sought in the parks, but bass and even an occasional walleye turn up.

0. Other Places - You will locate more places where you can cast a line if you do a little searching on your own. Many marinas don't mind a quiet fisherman in an out-of-the-way spot. There are private piers, too, where there might be a small charge. Sometimes a friendly request will bring a go-ahead. So find a likely place, bait up with shiners or worms, and send your offerings deep. You'll find you can bank on Lake Erie.

Anglers often do well from the many piers and docks along the Lake Erie shore.

35

Start the engine, sit back, relax and let's go fishing.

Fishing Lakes Forecast

By Jim Robey

Grab the fishing rods and tackle. Hook up the boat. Let's go fishing.

And don't forget to take the Ohio Fishing Guide. It will lead you to the best fishing in the Buckeye State.

In one trip, or even with a number of them, we wouldn't have time to visit all the inland lakes, but here are examples of some that should be on our itinerary.

Starting in the northwest corner of the state, we can't pass up La Su An Wildlife Area where the 13 ponds and small lakes intensely managed by the wildlife division produce some of the best bass and bluegill fishing in Ohio.

By contrast, in the northeast corner of Ohio, Pymatuning Lake sprawls across the Ohio-Pennsylvania line. It presents a totally different fishing environment.

At Pymatuning, 14,650 acres of water offer the best walleye fishing of an inland lake in Ohio. Although walleyes are stocked on the Pennsylvania side of the reservoir, it's a natural fishery in Ohio waters.

A fishing tour through eastern Ohio could take time. So many outstanding lakes beckon, including Leesville and Piedmont, two of the top musky lakes.

Clendening Lake, over the hill from Piedmont, is the premier lake in that region for bass fishing. Seneca Lake, east of Cambridge, is the only lake in Ohio with striped bass fishing.

Salt Fork Lake, also near Cambridge, is perhaps the best all-around fishing lake in the eastern half of the state. The 2,900-acre lake offers excellent crappie fishing, a good population of bass, walleyes, muskies and a healthy number of hand-size bluegills.

Further into southeast Ohio, Lake Rupert rates highly. Dave Bright, district fish management supervisor in that part of Ohio says, "It's one of those lakes where everything we've done seems to have worked."

The result is excellent fishing for bass, a strong population of channel catfish and up-and-coming saugeye fishing.

In central Ohio, Alum Creek Lake north of Columbus deserves attention. Fish management practices are working there, too.

Steve Graham, district fish management supervisor in that area, said, "The goal at Alum is to provide saugeye fishing unrivaled in the district."

Along with it, Alum has a good population of 6- to 8-inch bluegills, lots of crappies from 8 to 12 inches, largemouth and smallmouth bass and musky fishing that is coming on rapidly.

Alum, and any other lake in Ohio, still can't match Indian Lake near Bellefontaine when it comes to the saugeye. Indian Lake has become the "saugeye capital of the world," as rated by Ohio Fishing Guide. It offers outstanding bass fishing as well, plus excellent fishing for catfish.

Our brief make-believe tour ends at Grand Lake St. Marys, the best crappie lake in Ohio - was, is and probably will continue to be the number one crappie spot in the state. Yellow perch and catfish have been trying to create more attention than crappies are getting at Grand, but they can't quite do it.

These are just a few of about 65 inland bodies of water reviewed in detail. As you travel to them you'll note that some of the large lakes in Ohio still limit motor size to 10 horsepower, if not electric motors.

You need more than one boat to fish Ohio properly, or friends who own rigs different from the one you have. Good luck.

Calvin Pyle casts for muskies at Clear Fork Reservoir.

37

John Schiller, at Indian Lake, samples the best saugeye fishing in Ohio.

District 1, Lakes in Central Ohio

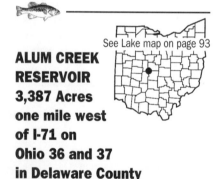

See Lake map on page 93

ALUM CREEK RESERVOIR
3,387 Acres
one mile west
of I-71 on
Ohio 36 and 37
in Delaware County

Anglers in central Ohio can be optimistic about fishing prospects at Alum Creek Lake north of Columbus.

With saugeye fishing on the rise, smallmouth and largemouth bass to entice anglers, crappies of quality size and some of the fastest growing muskies in the state, Alum Creek has a lot to offer.

The saugeye made its debut at Alum Creek in 1987 when 200,000 of the fin-gerling hybrids were stocked. In recent years, the number planted annually has been increased to 300 per acre when fish hatcheries can supply that many. Normal stocking of the saugeye is a third that number.

"What we want to do at Alum Creek is create a lake with unrivaled saugeye fishing," says Steve Graham, district fish management supervisor in central Ohio.

Indications the biologists are succeeding are apparent in the names of favorite saugeye fishing spots, such as Crisco Point. It is said saugeye action is so hot at Crisco Point anglers stock their pantry with cooking oil before they go to Crisco Point (see Alum Creek map).

Other saugeye places include the Williams Lake area, long, shallow flats and the drop-offs next to the flats and off the points.

Elmer Heyob, assistant district fish

management supervisor, is delighted with the muskies in Alum Creek. Muskies have been stocked since 1990 at a rate of one per acre.

Although excessive rainfall last spring is blamed for washing a number of these fish out of Alum Creek Lake, the outlook remains good for taking super-large muskies.

"The growth rate for muskies has been excellent. A five-year-old female musky may be 48 inches in length," Heyob said.

Alum Creek Lake is a 3,400-acre, flood-control lake with a variety of fish habitat. Long and narrow, the headwaters feature cliffs, drop-offs and points that present choice spots for bass.

The total bass population, considered fairly good, consists of more largemouth bass than smallmouth, but with good numbers of both. The minimum size limit for bass is 12 inches.

Bluegills at Alum are plentiful in the 6- to 7-inch range, and smaller. Those who know the lake can fill a fish basket with these panfish.

Crappie fishing should please anglers. Alum used to have a tremendous number of 7- to 8-inch, paper-thin crappies, but the size has improved.

Crappies up to 12 inches have become fairly common.

Channel catfish are abundant. A number of channels from 10 to 15 pounds are available to anglers.

Alum Creek has a marina and one of the finest campgrounds in the state. Bait and tackle stores are on nearly every road leading to the reservoir.

See Lake map on page 95

**Buckeye Lake
3,800 Acres
off I-70
about 25 miles
east of Columbus in
Fairfield, Perry and
Licking counties**

Largemouth bass, hybrid striped bass and catfish are the fish that immediately come to mind when you think of Buckeye Lake, the 3,800-acre canal lake near Hebron.

Now you can add saugeyes to the list. The developing, saugeye program at Buckeye is ready to be cultivated.

A Rent-A-RV trailer at Alum Creek State Park offer the comforts of home on a lake with excellent fishing

This hybrid was introduced in 1993 at the popular recreation lake and, in years since then, annual deposits of 100 fingerling saugeyes per acre have been made.

The walleye-sauger cross has done well. You can expect to catch saugeyes from 22 to 24 inches, and bigger.

Besides the growing saugeye fishery through 1997, '98, '99 and beyond, anglers can anticipate continued fishing for the hybrid striped bass, plus decent bass fishing and world-class fishing for channel catfish and flatheads.

"When we set trap nets at Buckeye Lake we can hardly lift them because of the big shovelhead (flathead) catfish," said Elmer Heyob, assistant fish management supervisor in central Ohio.

"Catfishing is an under appreciated fishery at Buckeye Lake," Heyob said.

The hybrid striped bass, a cross between a female striper and a male white bass, was introduced at the lake in 1989. Experimental stockings have included fingerling-size hybrids and up to a million fry released in 1995 and '96.

Biologists have concluded that it is more practical to stock fingerlings, even if the initial cost is greater.

Buckeye is an early season lake because it is shallow and warms quickly in the spring. Besides a fast start for bass fishing, Buckeye is a good lake for crappies and yields lots of bluegills from 6 to 8 inches.

An angler could not find a better place in central Ohio to test dough ball recipes. Shallow and highly vegetated Buckeye Lake also has a world-class carp population.

Bass anglers use a lot of surface plugs, spinnerbaits, buzzbaits and artificial worms. A 12-inch minimum size limit applies.

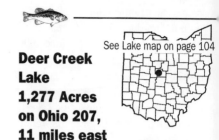

See Lake map on page 104

Deer Creek Lake
1,277 Acres
on Ohio 207,
11 miles east
of Washington Court House
in Pickaway County

Deer Creek Lake, midway between Dayton and Columbus, attracts anglers from both towns, as well as from Cincinnati and other Ohio cities.

As one of the top resort parks in the state, with a lodge, cabins, beach, golf, trails and an excellent campground, it's no surprise that Deer Creek State Park and its lake have become a center of attention for outdoor recreation.

Fishing is popular. Some would say you couldn't find a better place for catching the saugeye than Deer Creek Lake, or the tailwater pool below the reservoir.

Deer Creek is where the saugeye, a cross between the sauger and walleye, was first tested in an Ohio lake. From that highly successful experiment the saugeye program has grown to the planting of 10 million saugeyes a year in 58 bodies of water.

At Deer Creek, the fish still rates the highest priority with an annual stocking of 500 fingerlings per acre for the last three years, as compared to 100 per acre for most reservoirs.

"The Deer Creek tailwater area gets a lot of fishing pressure during the winter. On milder days, from 50 to 75 people will be fishing for saugeyes," said Steve Graham, district fish management supervisor.

In the lake itself, some of the better places to fish for the hybrid are off the point at Tick Ridge, the drop-offs around other points, flats and sandy areas. In the spring of the year, the riprap shoreline at the dam is a good place to fish.

Largemouth bass, crappies, channel catfish and white bass are other species to target. A 12-inch minimum size limit applies to bass that can be found in average numbers.

White bass are plentiful. Locate a school of them and you can have fun pulling in one after another. They'll take jigs with twisters, spinners, smaller crankbaits and minnows.

The fluctuating water level at this flood-control lake and an annual winter drawdown of more than 10 feet make it impossible to predict what the crappie fishing will bring from one year to the next. Some seasons are good, and some are not.

Catfishing is something you can depend on. Try fishing with cut shad in the creek channel in the upper end of the lake, fishing experts advise.

As a busy park lake, you will find heavy boating traffic on weekends during the summer. You'll enjoy the lake more on weekdays if you can schedule

Delaware is the only lake in Ohio with a minimum size on crappies (9 inches).

your visit for that time.

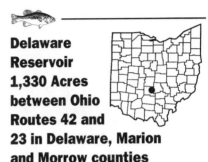

Delaware Reservoir 1,330 Acres between Ohio Routes 42 and 23 in Delaware, Marion and Morrow counties

Delaware Lake, north of Columbus, is the first lake in Ohio with a minimum size limit on crappies. Although it was started on March 1, 1991, Delaware remains the only lake with a size limit on crappies.

The size limit, as of the 1997 fishing season and until further notice, is 9 inches. Originally it was 10.

Biologists adjusted the size because the lake has a strong population of crappies, a good growth rate for the fish and too many crappies in the 9- to 10-inch range that were not being harvested.

While the idea of a size limit on crappies has not spread to lakes elsewhere in the state, it has been discussed.

Some crappie anglers, who seem to like the idea of a size limit on crappies, drive from other parts of Ohio to fish at Delaware Lake.

Steve Graham, district fish management supervisor in central Ohio, modestly points out that he isn't so sure the size limit has made Delaware the "great" crappie lake these people are claiming.

"Sometimes a regulation like this will cause a certain lake to receive more attention," Graham said.

A fish that should be getting more

respect at Delaware is the saugeye, a fish largely overlooked because of the interest in crappies, white bass, largemouth bass and the excellent population of channel catfish.

The saugeye was first stocked in 1986. In recent years, annual plantings of saugeyes at a rate of 100 per acre have produced a stable population of the hybrid. The fish can be taken from the lake, or in the tailwater area after the lake is lowered at the end of the recreation season.

"This fishing is a sleeper. In late fall, some fishermen hammer the saugeyes on the points in Delaware Lake," says Elmer Heyob, assistant district fish management supervisor.

Although Delaware is a favorite lake for holding bass fishing tournaments, the bass population is average. One attraction is the amount of structure. Delaware has tree stumps, submerged creek channels, shoreline cover and plenty of drop-off areas. The minimum size limit on bass is 12 inches.

The flood-control reservoir was filled in 1950. Boats with motors of unlimited horsepower can be used on the 1,330-acre lake with good boat ramps and a state campground.

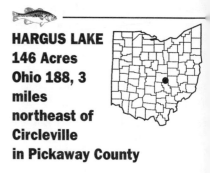

HARGUS LAKE
146 Acres
Ohio 188, 3 miles northeast of Circleville in Pickaway County

Hargus Lake in A.W. Marion State Park has a new look since the accidental introduction of the zebra mussel. Yes, it's the same mollusk that invaded the Great Lakes in 1986.

Just as the zebra mussel spread rapidly in Lake Erie, it has done so at Hargus. And as at Lake Erie where the algae-eating zebra has made the water clearer, it has done the same at Hargus Lake.

No one knows for sure exactly how the zebra mussel was transported from Lake Erie to little, 146-acre Hargus Lake in central Ohio, but it probably was carried by someone's boat, motor or other

Hargus Lake is a quiet, dependable place for catching small bass and panfish.

tem of equipment used at the Great Lake.

Clearer water at Hargus has resulted in less vegetation, a deeper thermocline in the summer and a flourishing population of small crappies, small bluegills and small bass.

The 15-inch size limit on bass was established to help reduce the numbers of small panfish. It has provided good catch-and-release bass fishing, but it also means one must devote more time to bass in order to catch a bass large enough to keep.

Hargus was drained in 1985, rough fish were removed and game fish were placed in the lake. It was a successful fish-management project at the time.

Muskies were stocked in 1987, '88 and '89. Returns on muskellunge have not been good and the stocking was discontinued. Very few remain.

Hargus is a quiet, inviting lake where an angler has a good chance of catching small fish in a pleasant setting. The lake has a boat ramp and electric motors are allowed.

**HOOVER
RESERVOIR
3,843 Acres
off Sunbury
Road, about
15 miles north of
downtown Columbus in
Delaware and
Franklin counties**

The 10-horsepower limit on motors Hoover Lake may be a sore point for a number of pleasure boaters in central Ohio, but most anglers aren't complaining.

At Hoover, no speed boats are racing by you. No skiers are running between you and the bank. No jet skiers are buzzing you. And you won't spend the day bouncing around in wake from passing boats. Hey, mom, you'll like this place!

Large numbers of fish inhabit Hoover Lake, although some anglers may have a hard time believing it. The reservoir can be frustrating at times because of changing water levels. Hoover supplies water for the city of Columbus and the water level may fall severely during a drought.

Hoover used to be the best place in central Ohio for walleyes, but that fish has been replaced with the saugeye, the cross between a sauger and walleye.

In 1988, Hoover was stocked with 150,000 fingerling saugeyes and 235,000 were added in '89 and 430,000 in '90. Survival was good.

Since then, saugeyes have been stocked yearly at a rate of 300 per acre when the quota has been met by the fish hatcheries.

State fishery biologists look for excellent saugeye fishing in 1997, '98, '99 and beyond. It is recommended that anglers seek out these fish on the flats and the drop-offs along the flats, of which there are many at Hoover Lake.

Smallmouth bass are taken in the lower basin and largemouth bass are found throughout the lake, near shoreline cover. Hoover does not receive heavy pressure on its bass population because of the 10-horse restriction on motors. A minimum size limit of 12 inches applies.

Hoover is considered a good spring crappie lake. "Try minnows or jigs in the middle or upper basins around shoreline cover," biologists say.

Channel catfish and white bass are taken at Hoover. The lake also has a good population of 6- to 8-inch bluegills.

Bow hunters can have a good day taking carp in the reservoir's shallow marshes in the spring.

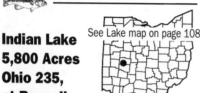

Indian Lake
5,800 Acres
Ohio 235,
at Russells
Point in
Logan County

See Lake map on page 108

Biologists across America are calling Ohio the "saugeye capital of the world."

If that's true, Indian Lake would have to be the "saugeye fishing capital of the world."

About 10 million saugeyes are produced at Ohio fish hatcheries for stocking every year at 58 locations and none of them is more productive than Indian Lake.

Limit catches of saugeyes are taken after the ice breaks up. Good fishing continues through spring. In the summer, other fish rate more attention.

Then, as the water cools in the fall, the saugeyes are back. More limit catches pile up. Indian Lake freezes and ice fishermen take saugeyes through the ice.

Where do they all come from?

"What made the difference for us at Indian Lake is when we increased our hatchery production and were able to stock fingerling saugeyes instead of the fry we put in during 1988 and '89," says Steve Graham, district fish management supervisor in central Ohio.

Since 1990, the wildlife division has been stocking from 200,000 to 600,000 fingerling saugeyes per year at Indian. Usually, it's the latter number. The results have been amazing.

At times it seems that 10 saugeyes from 15 to 22 inches show up for every fingerling planted. No way, explained Graham. The biologist contends he is pleased with 10 percent survival on stocked fish. Some saugeyes up to eight pounds, and bigger, have been taken at Indian Lake.

Saugeye hotspots include the feeder canal at Moundwood, the deep hole at the end of the canal and the area south of Dream Bridge. Anglers cast, drift, or troll slowly with jig and twisters fished just off bottom. Tipping the bait with a

Dan Henkle (left) and Shawn Jordan sharpen bass-fishing skills for MDA Tournament at Indian Lake.

minnow often increases the catch.

Old timers at Indian say the bass fishing is getting better, and results of bass fishing tournaments over the last three years prove that's true. Graham says there is no reason why a larger saugeye population would benefit bass.

"At Indian, I think we are dealing with a lake where water quality has been improved greatly and the lake can support more fish," Graham said.

Besides the no-till farming practices that have reduced the amount of silt washed into Indian Lake, septic tanks around the lake are being replaced with sewers connected to a modern waste treatment facility.

Excellent bass fishing is expected at Indian in coming seasons, as well as good fishing for crappies, bluegills, bullheads and channel catfish. White bass also may be taken.

Some of the biggest largemouth bass caught every year will be pulled in during the months of March and April.

Indian Lake is an amazing body of water. Thousands of people can be pleasure boating, skiing and swimming at one end of the reservoir. At the same time, at the other end of the reservoir, in a spot known as "Old Game Refuge," an angler can be fishing in solitude.

A sense of isolation is felt as the angler probes the channels and potholes of the marsh amid the expanse of cattails, lily pads and button bush. Here you will see ducks, geese, herons, blackbirds and dozens of other species of marsh-dwellers.

This, too, is the place for bass, and it is where anglers begin searching for largemouth in early spring.

Indian Lake has marinas, bait stores, launching ramps, camping and private rental cabins.

Kiser Lake
380 Acres
Route 235
near St. Paris
in Champaign County

At Kiser Lake a new fish is providing anglers with big-game fishing thrills at a quiet, body of water in rural Ohio.

It's the wiper, a cross between a female white bass and male striped bass. Biologists refer to is as "the reciprocal."

By reciprocal, they mean the reverse cross of a more familiar fish, the hybrid striped bass. That hybrid is produced in a fish hatchery by crossing a female striped bass with a male white bass.

Hybrid stripers are stocked at East Fork Lake near Cincinnati and at a few other lakes in Ohio.

The wipers are being tested at Kiser Lake, much to the delight of the anglers who have caught them. Once on the line, this fish provides an impressive battle.

Stocking of the wipers at Kiser began in 1992. Some of the fish have attained impressive size. Seven to nine pounders have been caught, according to fishing reports.

"We stocked 9,400 in 1992 and have continued nearly every year with additional plantings at a rate of 25 hybrids per acre," said Steve Graham, district fish management supervisor in central Ohio.

The fish are set free in June when they are about one inch long.

Other fish at Kiser include a good

population of largemouth bass, bluegills from 6 to 8 inches, many channel catfish and a goodly number of crappies from 7 to 9 inches.

Saugeyes have not been stocked since 1991. Any survivors from that planting would be quite large.

Kiser is overlooked by many anglers because of its ban on motors - even the electrics are not allowed. The lake was deeded to the state with the no-motor stipulation.

Bass anglers familiar with Kiser fish the underwater stumps. Many are visible along the north side. Others you've just got to know about.

Kiser rarely becomes too roily to fish. When other lakes are muddy, Kiser can be counted on for its clear, spring-fed water.

A state-leased marina offers bait, tackle and rental boats from spring through fall.

KNOX LAKE
495 Acres
off Ohio
Route 95,
near Fredericktown
in Knox County

Knox Lake is the first lake in Ohio managed for trophy bass fishing. An 18-inch minimum size limit on bass went into effect on March 1, 1991.

"It has made Knox Lake one of the top trophy-bass fishing places in the state," says Steve Graham, district fish management supervisor in central Ohio.

The 495-acre lake between Mt.

Vernon and Mansfield was a logical choice for this decision. Knox was one of the first lakes in the state with an experimental size limit on bass adopted in 1983. Fishing improved dramatically.

Of 60 water areas fished in 1995 by tournaments sanctioned by the Ohio Bass Chapter Federation, Knox Lake rated first in bass fishing. It produced the highest catch rate per hour, according to a joint study by the Bass Federation and the Division of Wildlife.

At Knox Lake the bass catch per hour rate was .61, or a fish for every 1.6 hours of fishing. Of these bass, two out of three were 12 inches or larger. No record was kept on the amount of time needed to catch an 18-inch bass.

Other water areas in the list of top bass fishing places included Portage River, where 2.2 hours were needed to catch a bass; Sandusky Bay, 2.3 hours and O'Shaughnessy Reservoir, 2.3 hours.

Knox should be equally as good for taking bass this year, and for years to come.

Bluegill fishing is decent, crappies are recovering from a slump and the fishing outlook for channel catfish is outstanding. Channels up to 10 pounds are in Knox Lake and the best time to get them is while fishing at night.

Creel studies conducted in 1981 and 1982 at Knox revealed anglers were removing about 1,200 bass from the lake annually. A 16-inch size limit was established to reduce the harvest.

The first year the 16-inch limit was adopted only 63 keepers were taken. But anglers threw back 6,700 largemouth and the population of 12-inch bass more than doubled.

Since '84, Knox has been one of the hottest bass fishing lakes in the state, with anglers catching and releasing hundreds of 13- to 16-inch largemouth.

Advancing the minimum size limit to 18 inches in 1991 expanded catch and release fishing and gave Ohio anglers a place to count on for trophy bass.

Knox has cover, a good boat ramp and motors up to 10 horsepower are permitted. The lake is about 60 miles northeast of Columbus.

O'Shaughnessy Reservoir 920 Acres Ohio 257, four miles north of Dublin in Delaware County

This long, narrow reservoir on the Scioto River is one of the major fishing spots in central Ohio, yet one overlooked by many anglers. In a normal year, O'Shaughnessy has a good population of largemouth bass, a few smallmouth, bluegills 6-7 inches, fair numbers of white crappies, channel catfish and bullhead.

Bass tournament anglers like O'Shaughnessy, as proven by the two dozen or so events scheduled at the reservoir each year. Brush and fallen trees along the entire west bank receive heavy fishing pressure, yet they continue to give up fish.

A joint study by the Ohio Bass Chapter Federation and the Ohio Division of Wildlife in 1995 found that O'Shaughnessy ranked as the fourth leading bass producer in the state among 60 fishing areas checked.

Bass anglers at O'Shaughnessy fished 2.3 hours to catch a bass. The only spot significantly better was Knox Lake where 1.6 hours were required to take a bass.

The same survey found that for every bass caught that did not meet the state's minimum size limit of 12 inches at O'Shaughnessy, three bass were 12 inches or longer.

Saugeyes have been stocked at O'Shaughnessy since 1981. Annual plantings of the hybrid have continued at a rate of about 100 per acre.

Besides taking saugeyes in the lake, anglers do well on this fish at the tailwa-

Bass anglers at O'Shaughnessy Reservoir do well with their tournaments and release the fish they catch.

ter pool from December through February. Survival of recent year classes has been excellent and should mean anglers can expect excellent saugeye fishing in the next few years.

A good ramp at Home Road on the east side of the reservoir affords easy access for anglers and pleasure boaters. During the summer months, boat traffic is heavy from about 10 a.m. to dark. Anglers who get on the water at daybreak won't have too much competition.

The city of Columbus maintains the facility and provides convenient access along the east bank for people who want to fish from shore or enjoy a family picnic.

Rush Creek Lake
309 Acres
13 miles northeast
of Lancaster off Ohio 22 on County Road 74 in Fairfield and Perry counties

When the boat traffic gets too heavy at Buckeye Lake an alternative is not far away. Just a 10-mile drive from Thornville on the south side of Buckeye is 309-acre Rush Creek Lake, a quiet spot for fishing.

Here, motors are limited to 10 horsepower.

Rush Creek, two miles east of Rushville, was completed in 1984 and is managed for fishing by the Ohio Division of Wildlife.

The lake has so many largemouth

bass from 8 to 15 inches the division has set a 12- to 15-inch slot limit, meaning bass from 12 to 15 must be released.

Anglers are being encouraged to keep bass less than 12 to reduce the population and help create a quality bass fishing area with a higher percentage of larger bass. The slot also permits keeping bass longer than 15 inches.

Having more of the larger bass in a lake does more than add to the quality of bass fishing. It also can mean thinning out the numbers of runt-size, bait-stealing bluegills.

Although bluegills up to eight inches can be found at Rush Creek, they are greatly outnumbered by smaller 'gills. The crappies at Rush Creek Lake also could use some thinning. Average size for them is 6 to 8 inches.

The boat launching ramp at Rush Creek Lake lies off County Road 74. Standing trees and stumps can be found on both sides of the lake that runs east to west. The greatest amount of cover is found in coves on the south side of the reservoir.

Cleveland Perry and daughter know a small lake can yield a monster catfish.

There's no better place to fish than Lake Erie, says charter boat Captain Don Manning.

District 2, Lakes in Northwest Ohio

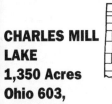

CHARLES MILL LAKE
1,350 Acres
Ohio 603,
5 miles east of Mansfield in Richland and Ashland counties

Charles Mill, stocked with saugeyes since 1989, has provided anglers with a dual fishery. The hybrid has done well in the lake and the tailwater pool below the dam is an excellent place to take saugeyes from November through March.

With fingerling saugeyes being planted yearly at a rate of 300 per acre, fishing for this popular species should remain strong through the 1990s. Saugeyes up to 8 pounds are possible and 3 to 5 pounders are common.

Charles Mill is one of the gem lakes in the Muskingum Watershed Conservancy District (MWCD). The lake itself affords good fishing for bass, crappies and catfish and fair numbers of bluegills are found.

Larry Goedde, fish management supervisor in northwest Ohio, says the outlook for crappies is good. The lake has white and black crappies ranging from 8 to 11 inches.

Bass anglers, who have been doing well at Charles Mill, may note a little decline in fishing as a result of the below average hatch in 1995 and '96. One good spawning season would restore the population. The minimum size limit for bass is 12 inches.

Charles Mill was designed as a flood-control lake serving a large watershed area. Turbidity can be a problem and you won't find the water as clear as at most of the other conservancy lakes.

A 10-horsepower motor restriction applies.

CLEAR FORK LAKE
See Lake map on page 100
944 Acres
Ohio 95, five miles southwest of Mansfield in Richland and Morrow counties

Clear Fork Lake is where anglers think muskies.

They have a good reason. The next fish that strikes the lures could well be a big, hard-fighting muskellunge.

Muskies are stocked at a rate of about 1,000 per year and they have done so well Clear Fork has become a leading producer in Ohio. The muskies are 8 inches to 10 3/4 inches long when stocked, and they grow rapidly in the Clear Fork water.

In 1996, biologists say, Clear Fork was number one in Ohio by yielding the highest reported catch of muskies 30 inches and over.

It is not uncommon at Clear Fork for an expert angler to catch two or three muskies in one day. What makes this possible is that most of these experts are die-hard musky fans who release all the fish they catch, thus the great fishing for muskellunge at Clear Fork is recycled.

The 944-acre reservoir near Mansfield is a good all-around lake. It has an excel-

lent population of largemouth bass, fair fishing for bluegills and an average number of channel catfish in the 10- to 21-inch range. Bass anglers should remember that a 12-inch minimum size limit applies.

A plus for the coming seasons is the crappie outlook. Black and white crappies are in Clear Fork and their numbers are growing. Crappies up to 13 inches are possible, but 8 and 9 inchers are more plentiful.

White bass also are taken at the reservoir.

Clear Fork was constructed in 1950 to provide water to the city of Mansfield.

Besides good fishing, Clear Fork is a delightful spot for a family outing. The picnicking facilities are excellent.

A multi-lane boat ramp affords convenient access to the lake. Boats with larger engines may be used, but a 10 mph speed limit is strictly enforced. At Clear Fork, fishing is the name of the game.

Clear Fork Lake has an excellent population of crappies.

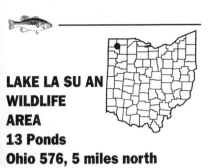

LAKE LA SU AN WILDLIFE AREA
13 Ponds
Ohio 576, 5 miles north of Montpelier in Williams County

Good fishing has been maintained at Lake La Su An Wildlife Area in northwest Ohio through a well balanced fish-management program by the Ohio Division of Wildlife.

Although catches of super-large bluegills at La Su An Lake are down slightly, the numbers of fish taken are up, according to Larry Goedde, fish management supervisor in northwest Ohio.

"We still see a lot of 8- and 9-inch bluegills taken by fishermen," Goedde said.

Goedde expects the size range of bluegills in La Su An to improve in 1998 and '99 as the bass population increases and a better ratio between the number of large bass and bluegills is achieved.

Some of the best bass fishing in the state can be experienced at the wildlife area. While it is not uncommon for an angler to catch 30 bass a day, most bass are protected by length limits and have to be released.

The intensely managed area produces about 5,500 angler use days on 136 acres of water. From April through June, about a third of the fishing requests can be accommodated. It is easier to get a reservation other times of the year.

Remember that failure to obtain a reservation on the requested date doesn't rule out fishing completely. Seven of the 13 lakes are open without reservation, but you must pick up a free, daily permit at the check-in station.

The 13 ponds on the 1,161-acre Lake La Su An Wildlife Area in the northwest corner of Williams County have the

Musky hunters Matt Foose and daughter, Rebecca, regard Clear Fork Lake as a top reservoir for musky fishing.

highest populations per acre of large-mouth bass of any lakes in the state, and a high percentage of the bluegills are 8 inches or larger.

Rules to limit the harvest of bass and bluegills are subject to change and may include size and bag limits, slot limits and catch-and-release fishing. La Su An fishing regulations are supplied to anglers who request a fishing date.

La Su An is the only inland area in the state with a daily creel limit on panfish. Although subject to change, there are minimum size and creel limits where designated.

Reservations are required at the lakes that are open from early April through October. Ice fishing is permitted for two or three weeks in January and February until the winter harvest quoto is met.

Usually, open water lake fishing is permitted on Thursday, Friday, Saturday, Sunday and Monday. Ice fishing is allowed on Thursday and Sunday, weather permitting.

Spring/summer reservations must be made by phone from 8 a.m.-noon Monday of each week for the five following fishing days. Anglers may call from 8 a.m.-noon on Friday to reserve any openings that may remain.

Ice fishing reservations are taken from 9 a.m. - noon on Monday for the following Thursday or Sunday.

Reservations will be accepted for no more than two people for each party, except for youth group reservations that can be more. Group fishing permits are issued for up to four people and each group must include at least one, but not more than two adults.

Only one reservation may be made for any three-week period on Lake La Su An or Lavere. There are no reservation frequency limits on the other lakes.

The number of reservations available daily for each lake: Lake La Su An, 12; Lake Lavere, 6; Lake Sue, 10; Lake Ann, 10; Lake Mel, 5; and Lake Us, 5.

No reservations are required at Lakes Hogback, Teal, Jerry, Clem, Wood Duck, Ed and Lou, but permits must be obtained at a check-in station on the property.

Outboard motors up to 10 horsepower may be used at Lake La Su An; only electric motors are permitted on other lakes and ponds which range from less than an acre to 82 acres.

The Division of Wildlife obtained the acreage from an estate in 1981 and intends to maintain the wilderness setting by limiting usage of the area.

The public hunting and fishing area is tucked away in the northwest corner of Williams County, not too far from Michigan and Indiana. Williams County Road R provides access from Ohio 576.

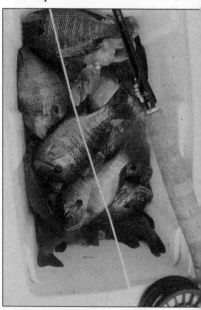

A good catch of large bluegills makes the day at La Su An.

PLEASANT HILL LAKE
850 Acres
off Ohio 603,
15 miles
southeast of Mansfield
in Richland and Ashland
counties

See Lake map on page 116

Bass fishermen should give Pleasant Hill Reservoir a try.

"It's a gorgeous lake," says Darrell Allison, retired fishery biologist for the Ohio Division of Wildlife.

The smallmouth bass has been one of Allison's favorite fish during his career, so we better listen up when he says "there may not be a better inland lake in Ohio for smallmouth."

Pleasant Hill, another in the chain of Muskingum Conservancy reservoirs, is two lakes in one. The upper portion is basically shallow while the lower end is deep with rocky shoreline and lots of cover. That's where you find the smallmouth.

Pleasant Hill also is an outstanding saugeye lake, dating back to the first planting of the hybrid in 1979. About 85,000 fingerling saugeyes are planted yearly.

Larry Goedde, Allison's successor as fish management supervisor in northwest Ohio, says 3- to 5-pound saugeyes can be expected and 7- to 8-pounders are possible.

The best places to fish for saugeyes are off the beach where anglers use twisters on jigs. Fishermen drift, or troll or jig vertically for the fish. Saugeyes

also are taken below the lake at the tailwater area in the fall.

The 850-acre lake also gives up crappies from 7 to 14 inches, in both the black and white variety, plus fair-to-middling numbers of bluegills and white bass. A run of white bass at the tailwaters can be expected in May.

Some muskies also have found a home in Pleasant Hill, as well as an occasional trout. Biologists explain the muskies apparently are washed from Clear Fork Lake and make their way 20 miles down the Clear Fork branch of the Mohican River into Pleasant Hill. Trout are stocked in Clear Fork River.

Mohican Lodge is on Pleasant Hill Lake. Although the lake belongs to the Muskingum Watershed Conservancy District, the lodge is operated by the Ohio Department of Natural Resources.

UPGROUND RESERVOIRS
total 2,000
Acres
in Northwest
Ohio at Findlay and Lima

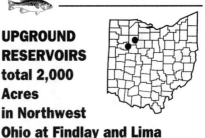

The upground reservoirs that provide water to Findlay and Lima have become a great asset to Ohio outdoors people who enjoy the sport of fishing.

Combined surface acreage of the lakes adds up to well over 2,000 acres. Some of the lakes afford good fishing in winter as well as summer, with saugeyes, walleyes and perch contributing to year around fishing.

The two reservoirs at Findlay go by the names of Reservoirs 1 and 2.

Findlay Reservoir No. 1 was built in 1950 and has a surface water area of 187 acres and an average depth of 24 feet with little cover. Electric motors only are permitted on the lake.

Findlay Reservoir No. 2 was constructed in 1968 with 827 surface acres of water and depths ranging from 16 to 33 feet. Boats with motors up to 10 horsepower are allowed.

The two reservoirs share a mile-long common dike southeast of Findlay, off Ohio Route 37 in Hancock County.

Findlay No. 2 is stocked with walleyes at a rate of 100 per acre. Natural reproduction of walleyes also has been recorded at upground reservoirs.

Perch have done so well at the upground lakes they don't have to be stocked. An exception is Findlay #2 where a decline in perch has been countered with the stocking of 200 perch per acre in 1995, 500 per acre in '96 and 1,000 per acre in '97, according to the plan.

Both of the lakes at Findlay have fair numbers of largemouth bass and bluegills, plus some exceptionally large channel catfish.

New London Reservoir, with 220 acres, two miles southwest of New London on Townline Road east off of Ohio 250, is another upground to remember if the walleye is your favorite fish.

The New London lake is stocked with walleyes and supports a good population of bluegills, channel catfish and an abundance of rock bass. The lake also has crappies, perch, smallmouth bass and largemouth bass.

Lima's hotspot upgrounds are Bresler (610 acres), Ferguson (305), Metzger (165), Lost (120) and Lima (85).

Of these reservoirs, walleyes are stocked at a rate of 100 per acre each year at Bresler and Ferguson while fingerling saugeyes are released yearly at Lost Creek, Lima and at 285-acre Willard Reservoir, two miles east of Willard on

Bresler and Ferguson are two of the Upground Reservoirs that feature walleye fishing.

Ohio 61.

There are good populations of perch and white bass in most of the upgrounds.

Walleyes are taken along wave-washed shorelines in the spring and by drift fishing or trolling during the summer and fall in the lakes where walleyes have been stocked. Yellow perch are found in the same areas.

Larry Goedde, district fish management supervisor, said moving along with an electric motor while trolling deep-running lures has been effective at Ferguson.

"We know two anglers at Ferguson who used this method and they caught eight walleyes that were 20 inches, or larger," Goedde said.

Bresler is regarded as the place to find super-large channel catfish that weigh up to 25 pounds, if not larger.

Balloon fishing is popular at the upgrounds.

Anglers use salt water reels and let out as much as 600 yards of line, fishing a live nightcrawler on a harness under the balloons while watching with binoculars.

The technique was started before boats were permitted on some of the upgrounds. At most of the larger lakes, boats now are allowed, a ramp is provided and balloon fishing continues.

Other upgrounds in northwest Ohio include Bucyrus No. 4 (150 acres).

Maumee River anglers return to their trailer with a load of river-run walleyes.

Melissa Hathaway, Sandusky, is delighted with the big sheepshead she catches at Lake Erie aboard Brownie's Delight.

District 3, Lakes in Northheast Ohio

**Atwood Lake
1,540 Acres
Ohio 542,
6 miles west
of Carrollton in Carroll and
Tuscarawas counties**

The saugeye remains one of the most promising fish to target as a result of a stocking operation that began at Atwood Lake in 1985.

With the exception of only one year since, fingerling saugeyes have been released annually at a liberal rate, including about 155,000 per year since 1995.

Saugeyes are plentiful from 14 inches in length up to 28 inches. The outlook for taking these fish is excellent.

Look for them on the flats, along the points and at the drop-offs.

The tailwater fishing below the dam has not been as productive as it is at some of the other lakes in Ohio, but it's worth a try during the winter months.

Before the saugeye was introduced, most of the attention at Atwood was directed to swimming, sailing, canoeing and pleasure boating. Motors up to 25 horsepower can be used at the reservoir that has 28 miles of shoreline.

District fish management supervisor Phil Hillman said .44 saugeyes per minute were caught while electrofishing several years ago. "That's above average, compared with other northeast Ohio lakes," Hillman explained.

Anglers can expect the saugeye angling to continue through the 1990s and into the 2000 years, based on what has already been placed in the lake.

Atwood has a good population of white and black crappies, and they have been on the upside of a cycle with respect to size. The average length is from 10 to 12 inches.

Anglers will catch them in the spring on minnows and jigs around brushy areas.

Other fish in the lake include bass, bluegills, catfish and carp. Hillman believes more people should try bass fishing. In his words, "The largemouth bass fishing is under utilized." The minimum size limit for bass is 12 inches.

Built in 1937 when a dam was constructed on Indian Fork, Atwood Lake has become the focal point of one of the most complete recreation parks administered by the Muskingum Watershed Conservancy District.

The popular family vacation center includes housekeeping cabins and the inviting Atwood Lodge, with guest rooms and restaurant. There is an excellent golf course, tennis courts, camping facilities, picnicking areas and hiking trails.

A complete marina with rental boats and bait and tackle serves boaters and anglers. There is no charge for use of the boat ramps at any of the Conservancy lakes.

Anglers set out on a misty morning in search of bass.

Berlin Lake 3,650 Acres U.S. 224, between Akron and Youngstown in Stark, Mahoning and Portage counties

Berlin is a flood-control and industrial water supply lake where the water level fluctuates up to 50 feet during the year.

Despite the ups and downs, Berlin produces a number of fish and has things going for it that cannot be claimed anywhere else in the state.

Berlin is the only lake in Ohio where natural reproduction of muskies has been documented, according to the Ohio Division of Wildlife.

"Moreover," says Phil Hillman, the fish management supervisor in northeast Ohio, "Berlin is the only lake in Ohio where there is natural reproducing of muskies, walleyes and smallmouth bass in the same body of water."

The Mahoning River, the stream feeding into Berlin Lake, was producing muskies even before the reservoir was filled in 1942.

Musky fishing has continued at Berlin without stocking. To protect this low-density population, a 40-inch minimum size limit on muskellunge was implemented in 1991 and continues. Most muskies caught fail to meet the minimum size requirement. In fact, only a few do.

A survey in 1982 revealed the annual bass catch was about 9,700 largemouth and 4,100 smallmouth. Over the years this ratio has reversed, with the smallmouth becoming the dominant species.

With its many rock cliffs, ledges, shoals and gravel bars, Berlin looks like a place to be when you want to catch the bronzebacks. Yet the outlook for bass fishing is rated "fair" and the minimum size limit for bass at Berlin is 12 inches.

Berlin is an annual producer of fairly good crappie fishing. Both black and white crappies can be taken at the reservoir. Biologists believe this fish is on the increase and raised the pre-season crappie fishing forecast from fair to good.

White bass in the 8- to 12-inch size range are plentiful at Berlin. Besides the lake, white bass fishing may be good at times in the fast water below the dam. Usually, this occurs in April and May, and the best lures are spinners, twisters, jigs and live minnows.

Walleye fishing is another bragging point. The annual harvest of walleyes should be good over the next couple of years as a result of at least two or three excellent hatches over the past five

springs.

Catches of walleyes 18 inches and larger will be common. The minimum size limit for walleyes is 15 inches.

Berlin has good boat ramps, and motors of unlimited horsepower are allowed.

Clendening Lake
1,800 Acres off Ohio 800, 12 miles south of Uhrichsville in Harrison County

Every section of the state needs a best largemouth bass lake, and this could be it for the northeast part of Ohio.

Phil Hillman of Akron, wildlife district three fish management supervisor, rates it very high.

Clendening Lake - a top bass lake then and now. Circa 1955, George Robey and son, Jim, bring home the fish.

"This is one of the best bass fishing lakes with excellent numbers of fish ranging from 12 to 23 inches," Hillman said.

Hillman remembers well a survey of the Clendening bass population by elec-trofishing. More than 2,000 bass were taken and released in six nights. Some of the fish were up to 24 inches.

The long, narrow lake winding through picturesque, tree-covered hills provides a delightful setting. And there is plenty of structure in the form of bays, brushy shorelines, points, rocky areas and some weedbeds.

Still, it appears that anglers are not taking advantage of the bass as well as they might. The lake does not receive a lot of fishing pressure because of the 10-horsepower limit on motors.

Other fish at Clendening include white crappie, bluegill, channel catfish and big flathead catfish. Creel surveys counted 124 flatheads that averaged 36.6 inches.

The lake was stocked with 98,602 fingerling saugeyes in 1990 for the first introduction of the hybrid. Saugeye releases have continued most years. None was stocked in 1995, but planting resumed in '96.

Over the next few years, anglers should take a number of these hybrids ranging from 15 to 24 inches.

The Muskingum Conservancy District has maintained the land around Clendening in its scenic, natural state. There is a full-service marina with bait, tackle and rental boats, plus a camp-ground and boat launching facilities.

Bass anglers should remember that 12 inches is the minimum size limit for keeping bass at Clendening Lake.

Highlandtown Lake
170 Acres
off Ohio 39
or 164,
10 miles south of Lisbon in Columbiana County

Highlandtown is a smaller lake situat-ed within the Ohio Division of Wildlife's Highlandtown Wildlife Area. Anglers who appreciate fishing in a scenic and quiet setting like this place. Electric trolling motors are allowed, but com-bustion engines are not.

Largemouth bass, bluegills, white crappies, black crappies, brown bull-heads, yellow perch and channel catfish are present in the lake.

Phil Hillman, district three fish man-agement supervisor in northeast Ohio, speaks highly of Highlandtown.

Hillman rates the fishing as good for all the species mentioned with the exception of two. His fishing forecast for bluegills and channel catfish is excel-lent.

"Bluegills ranging from 7 to 9 inches are not uncommon," Hillman says.

Although the lake has some trophy bass up to 8 pounds, a person who is not fond of catch-and-release fishing may want to go elsewhere. Highlandtown has a huge population of bass that don't meet the 15-inch mini-mum size limit.

The minimum size limit on bass, along with control of aquatic vegetation, has allowed predator fish to bring the lake into better balance with food supply. That appears to be the reason for the excellent bluegill fishery.

Crappie and yellow perch beckon anglers, but fishing for these species is secondary to angling for bass and bluegills.

Lake Milton 1,687 Acres off I-76, 15 miles west of Youngstown, Ohio 54 at County Road 18 in Mahoning County

The Department of Natural Resources obtained Lake Milton from the City of Youngstown in 1987 and it became Ohio's 72nd state park.

Water rose slowly behind the dam in 1988 to about 800 acres and pool level was reached in '89.

Fishing has come on strong since then with a number of anglers seeking muskellunge. The wildlife division received reports of 111 muskies caught in 1995 and 62 in '96. Of those taken in '96, 18 of the fish measured 42 inches or longer.

Biologists anticipate good fishing for crappies that average slightly under 9 inches and good fishing for bass.

The most recent creel survey found that the bass harvest was excellent at Milton Reservoir and the average size of the fish kept by anglers was 15.6 inches. Milton has a 15-inch minimum size limit for bass, and that includes smallmouth as well as largemouth.

A 15-inch size limit also applies to walleyes at Milton Reservoir. About 346,000 fingerling walleyes were

stocked at the lake in 1995 and nearly 170,000 in 1996.

When the state took possession of the park, Milton was stocked with 3.2 million walleye fry, 20,000 yearling channel catfish, 900 small muskies, 170,000 smallmouth bass less than 2 inches in length and more than 24,500 largemouth bass ranging from 3.5 to 7 inches.

Stocking has continued on a regular basis only for walleyes.

Boat owners will find two launching ramps at the lake, many places to fish from the shore and picnicking areas.

Ladue Reservoir 1,500 Acres U.S. 422 and Ohio 44, 30 miles east of Cleveland in Geauga County

The Ohio Division of Wildlife has been working to establish a strong population of walleyes in this 1,500-acre City of Akron water supply reservoir.

From the Ladue fishing forecast, it would appear the desired results have been achieved through annual plantings of walleyes that date as far back as 1983.

The 1995 and '96 releases of walleyes can be cited as examples. About 350,000 fingerling walleyes were set free over the two-year period.

These, along with walleyes from previous years, have created a solid population of walleyes with good numbers running at least 15 inches in length.

Other fish in the lake include an excellent population of channel catfish, numerous but small perch, bluegills, crappies and largemouth bass. The minimum size limit for bass is 12 inches.

A relatively shallow body of water, anglers will find a lot of trees, stumps and other structure to fish in the southern half of the reservoir. The north end of the lake is deeper.

Two boat ramps serve boat owners and only the electric type motors are allowed.

The City of Akron maintains a boat rental and restrooms, and requires anglers to have a permit. The permit can be obtained at the boat house, on Valley Road, east of Washington Street, a half mile east of State Route 44.

For the most current fishing report, also visit a bait and tackle store close to the lake. Several are near Ladue Reservoir.

Leesville Lake
1,000 Acres
Ohio 332,
5 miles south
of Carrollton in
Carroll County

Leesville, one of the most scenic lakes in Ohio, rates high on the list of the top places in the state for catching the mighty muskellunge.

"The total muskellunge catch reported in 1996 was 519 muskies, of which 40 were 42 inches or more," said Phil Hillman, district fish management supervisor.

Hillman says an additional 1,000 muskies that averaged 9.4 inches were stocked the same year. These, with similar plantings from previous years, will mean a strong musky fishing program through the 1990s and beyond.

Leesville Lake has been a consistent producer of muskellunge for many years, and usually rates as good or better than Pymatuning Lake, Rocky Fork, Piedmont, Clear Fork or any of the other musky lakes one cares to mention.

Three types of aquatic vegetation in the lake - curlyleaf pondweed, milfoil and coontail - assures plenty of weedy habitat for the hard-fighting game fish.

Long and narrow, and bending in the rough shape of a horseshoe, Leesville has 27 miles of shoreline. Most of the shoreline is wooded.

Bass anglers love to plug the banks and often get good results. Prime months for taking largemouth are April through June, September and October.

Leesville and several other Muskingum lakes put emphasis on fishing with a 10-horsepower motor limit.

The fishing outlook for bass is very good with 20 percent of the largemouth over 15 inches in length. The minimum size limit for bass is 12 inches.

Crappies at Leesville attract many anglers during the spring months. Biologists think crappie fishermen will do well and the fish they catch may average better than 9 inches apiece.

Leesville has two concessions with bait, tackle and boat rentals. Campgrounds are at both locations.

Motors at Leesville are limited to 10 horsepower.

Mogadore Reservoir 1,000 Acres Ohio 43, 3 miles east of Akron in Portage County

Just one look at a Mogadore Lake map is enough to give an angler fishing fever.

From where the dam has backed up the Little Cuyahoga River since 1939, Mogadore bends and weaves with islands, shoals, points, bays and 19 miles of shoreline.

It's a quiet lake, too, because only electric motors are allowed.

Despite the ban on big engines, Mogadore is a popular place. A survey taken by the Division of Wildlife disclosed that fishing pressure from mid-April to October is surprisingly heavy.

A comparatively shallow body of water, Mogadore is extremely clear and heavily vegetated with coontail and milfoil.

The clear water often requires using lighter line that is less visible to fish, particularly on bright days when there is little or no wind.

A primary fish at Mogadore is the bluegill, although the average size for this panfish is 6 inches. The redear sunfish at Mogadore grows much larger. Redears are better equipped to consume snails and fingernail clams, a source of food for the panfish.

Black and white crappies are plentiful, but average size is only 8 inches.

Fishing for brown bullheads is excellent with a large population of the whiskered bottom feeders running from 11 to 13 inches.

Mogadore yields a fair number of bass, including some that are five pounds or larger. Bass of typical size - 12 to 15 inches - are not as plentiful as biologists would like and that's why Mogadore has only a "fair" rating as a bass fishing reservoir.

The minimum size limit for bass at this lake is 12 inches.

Anglers can find catfish at nearly every lake in the state.

Three parking lots and a launching ramp serve visiting anglers. The City of Akron maintains two family camping areas, a swimming beach and picnic areas.

A fishing pier for handicapped anglers is off Ohio 43 near the Akron Watershed Office.

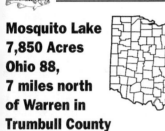

Mosquito Lake
7,850 Acres
Ohio 88,
7 miles north
of Warren in
Trumbull County

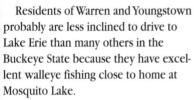

Residents of Warren and Youngstown probably are less inclined to drive to Lake Erie than many others in the Buckeye State because they have excellent walleye fishing close to home at Mosquito Lake.

Fishery folks rate Mosquito and Pymatuning Lake as the two best inland lakes in Ohio for walleyes.

During spring and fall, it's common to find big walleyes in shallow water at Mosquito.

Based on surveys, Mosquito Lake anglers catch more than 60,000 walleyes a season and keep approximately 50 percent of them. Of those taken home, the average fish is 13.7 inches long.

Well, maybe that's not up to Lake Erie standards, but it's better fishing than you can find at other inland lakes.

"Good numbers of 14- to 18-inch walleyes are available and most of the better walleye fishing occurs from mid-April to early June," says Phil Hillman, district fish management supervisor in northeast Ohio.

The wildlife division is serious about keeping Mosquito's reputation as the great inland lake for walleyes. It stocked 19 million walleye fry in 1995 and more than 12 million in '96 as part of an ongoing fish management program.

Studies have shown that the walleye population at Mosquito is 69 percent stocked fish and 31 percent from natural reproduction. Millions upon millions of walleye fry have been set free at Mosquito Lake since 1990.

Mosquito Lake has more northern pike than most people would believe. Although the reservoir never was stocked with northerns, some of the pike are trophy size.

The best spot for northerns is the waterfowl refuge, and that may explain why more pike aren't taken. The refuge is off-limits to fishing and hunting.

Black and white crappies inhabit the lake. Though not present in great numbers, crappies average a respectable 10 inches.

Bluegills average from 7 to 9 inches, which is better than most lakes. The size, along with the decent numbers, earns an excellent rating for Mosquito Lake bluegill fishing.

As for bass, there are better places. Based on creel surveys, the average take-home bass measures 13.2 inches. The minimum size limit for bass is 12 inches.

One thing to consider when going to Mosquito Lake is weather. This is a huge, relatively shallow body of water that can become dangerously rough when the wind picks up.

Army engineers built Mosquito in 1944 as a flood-control and water-supply lake.

Motors of unlimited horsepower are permitted and the lake attracts pleasure boaters and water skiers. The state park has boat ramps, camping, picnicking, hiking trails and swimming.

Nimisila Reservoir 811 Acres off Ohio 93, 6 miles south of Akron in Summit County

When the ice moves out, it's time for anglers to move in at Nimisila, a lake built 50 years ago by the Ohio Department of Public Works to help assure a source of water in the Portage Lakes area.

Nimisila is a good place to make a move on largemouth bass. The lake has an abundance of bass 12 inches and up, according to an electrofishing survey in 1995 by the wildlife division.

Biologists found that, of those bass measuring more than 8 inches, 52 percent exceeded 12 inches and 7 percent were longer than 15 inches.

The minimum size limit to keep a bass at Nimisila Lake is 12 inches.

Saugeye is another fish to target. The hybrid produced in fish hatcheries by crossing the walleye with a sauger was first stocked in 1990. About 41,000 fingerlings were set free.

Other plantings of this fish have continued, including 82,000 fingerlings in 1996. The population has developed to where the average saugeye taken by

anglers measures 16 inches. The larger hybrids run up to 26 inches.

Other major species in the lake are bluegill, crappie and channel catfish.

Surrounded by county roads, there is easy access to the lake. But the shoreline along the northwest sector of the reservoir is closed to bank fishing.

A relatively shallow body of water, Nimisila has extensive weed beds. It is a relaxing place to fish, and one where only electric motors are allowed.

Parking lots, launching ramps and restrooms have been provided.

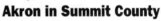

Portage Lakes 1,681 Acres Ohio 93 and 619, south of Akron in Summit County

A complex of five major lakes and with bays that also have names, the Portage Lakes is a recreation Mecca in northeast Ohio where thousands of people enjoy boating, picnicking and fishing. Most of the lakes are linked by channels.

Along the shore of the Portage Lakes are houses, summer cottages, boat docks, marinas and even shopping plazas.

While this is not the kind of setting most anglers envision when they think fishing, the lakes can be surprisingly productive.

Some people may have doubts as to whether fish are in the lakes, but the boys who know fishing and put in the time do well, according to local experts

The Portage system is one of the few places in Ohio where the angler can find chain pickerel. Long Lake, a member of the Portage complex, gave up the state record chain pickerel on March 25, 1961. Ronald Kotch of Akron caught the 26-inch, 6-pound fish.

Besides Long, Portage has North, East, West and Turkeyfoot lakes. The latter has been stocked with walleyes regularly, with the first planting going back to 1975. Walleyes also can be found in East and West lakes.

Saugeyes were introduced at Turkey Foot in 1988 with the planting of 2,158 fingerlings. A follow-up planting in 1990 resulted in the release of another 33,300 fingerling saugeyes. Since then saugeyes have been stocked regularly in the Portage system.

Largemouth bass are spread throughout the Portage lakes with Turkeyfoot serving as the favorite spot for many of the bass fans. Turkeyfoot is the deepest lake in the system. You would need an anchor line that is 50 feet long to touch bottom in some spots.

A 12-inch minimum size limit on bass applies at Turkeyfoot Lake.

Good crappie fishing generally occurs in the spring. Both the black and white varieties contribute to the creel.

Bluegills are plentiful, but the Portage Lakes contain a tremendous number of runt-size 'gills, along with bigger ones.

Brown bullheads from 11 to 14 inches add to the fishing, particularly in North Lake.

The Portage Lake boater and angler is never far from bait and tackle stores and marinas. While motors of unlimited horsepower are allowed, boat traffic is restricted in many areas by speed zones.

Punderson Lake
101 Acres
Ohio 87, 20 miles
east of Cleveland
in Geauga County

A natural pot-hole lake left by the glacier, Punderson is one of the more scenic bodies of water in Ohio. It's also one of the deepest, sliding to a depth of about 60 feet in the middle.

Punderson contains largemouth bass,

Walleyes at Pymatuning Lake reproduce naturally. A variety of weight-forward spinners will take them.

bluegills, catfish, crappies and perch.

The lake is stocked with trout. In recent years, the colorful golden trout has been the primary species stocked in early spring, if not sooner. The golden is a color variation of the rainbow trout.

Normal trout plantings each spring consist of about 2,500 "catchable" goldens. In this case, "catchable" has a dual meaning. The average size of these trout are a half-pound each, which makes them big enough to keep.

The fish also are "catchable" as they are vulnerable to anglers a day or so after they are released, if not the same day. Spinners such as the Rooster-tail, Mepps and Panther Martin are effective, as are small crankbaits and little spoons.

Berkley power bait works well, as do some of those old trout baits some people hate to hear mentioned - corn, Velveta cheese, miniature marshmallows and live worms.

Although trout can survive year around at Punderson Lake, most of the fish are taken within weeks after their

Walleye trollers need a selection of deep-running lures and a plug plucker to free one that gets snagged.

release.

Only electric motors can be used on boats and the lake serves as a focal point for one of the most complete state parks in Ohio.

Punderson has the first guest lodge opened in the state, plus vacation cabins, a golf course, hiking trails, campground and outstanding scenery.

The district wildlife office in Akron can provide you with trout stocking dates at Punderson, or at least give you an idea of when to expect them. Call 330-644-2293 to reach the office during business hours, Monday through Friday.

See Lake map on page 11

Pymatuning Lake
14,650 Acres
Ohio 85,
2 miles east of
Andover in Ashtabula County

It has been said carp are so thick in the refuge area of Pymatuning Lake that ducks walk on their backs.

All right, so Pymatuning has carp.

But anyone who thinks of Pymatuning only as a carp lake is missing out on a lot of fishing. This huge reservoir with 77 miles of shoreline splashing across the Ohio-Pennsylvania line has a tremendous number of game fish.

Fishery biologists in northeast Ohio rate Pymatuning as the best all-around lake in their part of the state. It could well be Ohio's most productive, inland body of water.

"Excellent numbers of walleyes

exceeding 15 inches should be available during April and May," says Phil Hillman, district fish management supervisor in northeast Ohio.

The walleye is number one on Pymatuning's fish list. Based on catch records, biologists say the average walleye at Pymatuning is 15.8 inches.

Fishing in 1995 concerned fish managers in that for every keeper walleye taken, six sub-legal fish were caught. Having to pull in six walleyes to get one big enough to keep was disappointing. A keeper at Pymatuning is 15 inches.

That ratio of throw-backs to legal-size fish is expected to improve, which led the wildlife division to elevate its preseason walleye fishing forecast at Pymatuning from good to excellent.

Not only does Pymatuning have walleyes in abundance, it has big ones - to 10 pounds or so.

What's so amazing about Pymatuning is that the fishing is natural. Walleyes are not stocked, or least they haven't been in recent years on the Ohio side. Pennsylvania began releasing walleye fry. As part of its continuing effort to supplement the walleye population, Pennsylvania released 2.5 million walleye fry in 1996.

May and June are two excellent months for walleyes. About the time walleye fishing is heating up at Lake Erie in late June and July, fishing goes flat at Pymatuning, but it picks up again after the water cools.

Surveys taken in Ohio and Pennsylvania indicate that the population of white and black crappie is up and anglers can expect to catch many crappies about 10 inches in length.

Don't forget the muskies. Some mighty big ones are cruising around the lake, although the catch rate is low. Only 17 were caught and reported to the wildlife division in 1996.

Bass anglers give Pymatuning a passing grade. A better lake for smallmouth than largemouth, the reservoir yields fair numbers of bass ranging from 10 to 18 inches.

Other fish at Pymatuning include perch, white bass and bluegills.

Special fishing regulations apply to the lake shared by Ohio and Pennsylvania. There are minimum size limits on walleye (15 inches), bass (12 inches) and musky (30 inches). Daily bag limits are 6 for walleye, 8 for bass and 2 for muskellunge.

Motor size is limited to 10 horsepower.

Tappan Reservoir 2,350 Acres along U.S. 250, 10 miles east of Uhrichsville in Harrison County

Tappan Lake is the kind of lake that appeals to bank anglers. It has more miles of accessible shoreline than any of the 10 lakes in the Muskingum Watershed Conservancy District.

U.S. 250, running parallel with the north shore, provides easy access to the bank that is protected by a riprap structure.

Having extolled the bank fishing, it must be added that Tappan has shortcomings. Crappies, while plentiful, are on the small side, from 6 to 8 inches.

The fishing outlook is much better for bass. Excellent numbers of 12-inch fish are available, based on electrofishing surveys by the Ohio Division of Wildlife.

Aquatic vegetation is limited, so look for bass around fallen trees and brush. Texas-rigged, weedless artificial worms and lizards will allow you to work this cover without getting snagged.

Bluegill fishing gets a decent rating. There are plenty of these panfish.

Channel catfish are abundant and average about 15 inches.

Saugeyes were stocked at Tappan Lake for the first time in 1990 when 118,000 fingerlings were set free. Biologists expected the fish to attain harvestable size in two years, which they did.

Follow-up plantings of saugeyes each year has provided a stable fishery. The annual stocking has been increased to 236,000 in 1995 and 235,000 in '96.

Saugeyes from 15 to 24 inches are in Tappan Lake. Furthermore, anglers can look forward to the coming saugeye fishing in 1998, '99 and beyond.

The Conservancy District has made many improvements around Tappan for campers, cabin renters, picnickers and other park users. A complete marina with bait and tackle supplies serves the public.

Overall, Tappan has become one of the most popular park lakes in the district.

Motors up to 120 horsepower are allowed.

See Lake map on page 12

West Branch Reservoir
2,350 Acres
Ohio 5, 5 miles east of Ravenna in Portage County

Weekends at West Branch are hectic because thousands of people converge at the popular park for camping, swimming, picnicking, pleasure boating and fishing.

That's why fishermen like to visit West Branch on a weekday, especially

Cabins at Tappan Lake are close to a reservoir where the saugeye fishing is getting better.

One swipe of a big plug like this at West Branch and you might have a musky or hybrid striped bass on the line.

when they can arrive at daybreak. Most pleasure boaters don't show until about 10 a.m.

The variety of habitat at the large lake is inviting for the angler. Curly pondweed affords habitat, as does shoreline cover and the old, sunken railroad bed, if you know where to find it.

Anglers also will find stumps, submerged timber and shoals at this flood-control reservoir built in 1965. The minimum size limit for bass is 12 inches.

West Branch is not all bass fishing. The lake has crappies, bluegills and catfish, plus two other species that can turn a dull day into a thriller with one swipe of a plug. Hybrid striped bass and musky are the heavyweights.

Hybrid striped bass average more than 16 inches. Biologists say that hooking a 25-inch hybrid is possible. Even larger ones are in the lake.

Muskellunge fishing is on a rebound from the 1995 fishing season when 11 muskies exceeding 20 pounds were caught by fishermen, according to the division.

In 1996, 30 muskies that exceeded 42 inches were taken. The total catch of

muskies in '96 was 192, compared to a total of 48 in '95. Two-year-old muskies at West Branch are from 20 to 24 inches long while the three- and four-year-olds are 30 and 33 inches, respectively.

The state record tiger musky was pulled from West Branch on Aug. 25, 1984, by James Prettyman of Suffield. The fish was 45 inches long and weighed 26 pounds, 8 ounces. Ohio has since dropped its tiger musky stocking program.

Biologists found that pure bred muskies do better in this state and that's the fish now released at West Branch. About 2,650 advanced fingerling muskies that measure nearly 10 inches apiece are stocked each year.

Fading from the fishing picture at West Branch is the saugeye. The fish was last stocked in 1992. Few of these hybrids remain, but if one of them was caught an angler would have a fish story to tell.

West Branch boat owners are served with two boat launching areas, one on the east side of the lake and the other is on the south.

Some of the finest bluegill fishing in
Ohio is found at lakes in southeast Ohio

District 4, Lakes in Southeast Ohio

**Burr Oak Lake
664 Acres
Ohio 13 & 78,
northeast of
Glouster in
Morgan and Athens counties**

Burr Oak Lake, with 665 acres of
water in 2,500-acre Burr Oak State Park,
is among the places in southeast Ohio
where an angler has a good chance of
catching trophy-size bass.

Chances are better that you'll locate
smaller bass because Burr Oak has an
abundance of them. That's why a 12- to
15-inch slot limit has been applied.

With the slot, you can keep bass less
than 12 inches or longer than 15. You
release the ones between 12 and 15.

Although the slot limit has been in
effect since 1988, the number of smaller bass remains higher than normal for a
lake the size of Burr Oak. It suggests
that most bass anglers are not willing to
keep smaller fish.

During summer months Burr Oak
may settle out and become extremely
clear. That may make it advisable for the
angler to use lighter line and smaller
lures.

Saugeyes have been stocked at Burr
Oak since 1988 and have been doing
fairly well. In recent years the planting
has consisted of 100 fingerlings per
acre.

Through the year, it is possible to
catch saugeyes on shad raps and other
deep-running lures. The choice locations
are close to the dam and the outer portion of the beach where the fish are
attracted to the sand bottom in 6 to 10
feet of water.

Catfish are plentiful with channels exceeding bullheads in numbers. On alternate years channel catfish are stocked in the fall at a rate of 25 per acre.

As for bluegills and redears, the sunfish can be found in average numbers, but slightly below average size.

Burr Oak Park is a choice place for family vacations. A lodge, cabins, camping, swimming beach and outstanding trails are major attractions. The boat ramp is fine and motors up to 10 horsepower are allowed.

Dillon Lake
1,660 Acres
Ohio 146
4 miles northwest
of Zanesville
in Muskingum County

Bass anglers can expect to find an ample number of fish at 1,660-acre Dillon Lake near Zanesville.

"We receive good reports on the bass fishing. The lake has many bass from 1 to 2 1/2 pounds," says Mike Greenlee, assistant fish management supervisor in the southeast wildlife district.

The lake has many bass that more than meet the minimum 12-inch size limit.

Saugeye fishing has been an attraction at Dillon since 1990, a year after the fish was introduced. The policy is to stock the lake each year with about 100 fingerling per acre and they've done well.

Growth rates of saugeye at Dillon

have been above average and it isn't uncommon to catch one of these hybrids up to 25 inches long.

Besides improved fishing in the lake, the fluctuating water level at Dillon has produced exceptional saugeye activity in the tailwater pool and on down the watershed to Zanesville where saugeyes may be taken under the Y Bridge.

Don't overlook the catfish. Channels are plentiful in the 8- to 25-inch range. Bluegill fishing is better than you'll find at most lakes.

Biologists find it hard to predict what the crappie fishing will bring from one season to the next because of the fluctuating water level. In recent years, crappies have been up and down.

The lake does have both the white and black crappie.

Motors of unlimited size are permitted on Dillon and boat owners will find good ramps. The state park at Dillon has hiking trails, swimming beach, campground and cabins.

Jackson City
Reservoir
(Hammertown
Lake)
190 Acres
Ohio 776, 2.5 miles west of
Jackson in Jackson County

The biggest fishing day of the year at Jackson City Reservoir, also known as Hammertown Lake, generally occurs the third Saturday in April when the annual trout derby is held.

About 4,000 keeper-size, golden or

71

rainbow trout are set free. Hundreds of anglers line the banks and fish from boats in a grand celebration of spring, trout and getting outdoors.

Jackson City Reservoir, a clear and deep body of water, has 190 surface acres. It's a choice place for the trout derby. The majority of fish are caught in the first few weeks after stocking, although it's possible for the trout to survive through the summer in the deeper portion of the reservoir.

Saugeyes have been stocked yearly since 1991 at a rate of 100 per acre. The chances of catching 15- to 18-inch saugeyes are good because the cold-water fish has adapted.

Bass fishing is less promising. Growth rates are below average in the clear water. An abundance of small large-mouth bass compete for the food source.

So far, a 12- to 15-inch slot limit since 1990 has failed to thin the number of smaller bass. Most anglers will not keep bass smaller than 12 inches and some won't take home a bass of any size.

Don't neglect the panfish. Bluegills and redear sunfish are well above average size for an Ohio lake. On a good day, an angler may take a basket full of seven-inch bluegills or perhaps a bluegill or redear up to 10 inches.

Channel catfish is another option. The lake is stocked on alternate years with channels. Some have attained the weight of 8 to 10 pounds.

The water-supply reservoir for the city of Jackson has a launching ramp. Electric trolling motors may be used.

Shore-fishing spots with inviting picnicking areas nearby can be found around the lake.

LAKE HOPE
120 Acres
Ohio 278, 3
miles north of Zaleski in
Vinton County

Lake Hope is as quiet and picturesque as any lake you could fish in Ohio.

Great bassin' cannot be promised, though. Electrofishing by state biologists show the largemouth bass population to be below average, although there are some decent bass in the reservoir and an occasional lunker is taken.

For years Lake Hope suffered from the acid water seeping out of old coal mines and running into the lake.

More than $1 million was spent by the state in sealing the mines. The water quality is better than it used to be, but still not up to the standard required for an outstanding fishery.

Channel catfish are doing well. Lake Hope is stocked with channels every other year at a rate of 25 fish per acre. The channels are from 8 to 12 inches when released in the fall.

An improved launching ramp with courtesy dock makes it easy to launch boats, including bass boats. Only electric motors can be used.

Lake Hope State Park in Zaleski State Forest is one of the prime recreation areas in southeast Ohio. Besides the lake for fishing and swimming, the park has a concession with rental boats, cabins, a summer lodge, campground and extensive trails for day hikes and backpacking.

LAKE KATHARINE
60 Acres
off U.S. 35
on 784 Rock Run Road in Jackson County

Lake Katharine, the most scenic body of water in the state, lies in 1,670-acre Lake Katharine State Nature Preserve. It is reached by turning south off U.S. 35, three miles west of Jackson, and following the signs on Rock Run Road to the preserve.

The Division of Natural Areas and Preserves manages the property to maintain its pristine qualities.

Bass and bluegills are the two primary species, but the lake also has crappies. A rule prohibiting the use of live minnows as bait has helped keep rough fish out of the lake.

A golden trout makes the day for this young man fishing Dow Lake near Athens.

The Lake Katharine fishing season is from April through October. In order to protect shoreline vegetation, fishing must be by boat, without gas or electric motor. The craft must be hand-carried or dragged 110 yards from the parking lot to the water.

Fishing is allowed four days per week (Friday, Saturday, Sunday and Monday) and no more than five boats can be put on the water on any one day. Reservations are made by calling the preserve the last Friday of the month prior to the month the angler wants to fish. The phone number is 614-286-2487. Calls are accepted from 8 a.m.-5 p.m.

April, May and June are the busiest months. Fishing dates usually are booked by 11 a.m. on the call-in day. September and October are two good months for fishing and there usually are vacancies at this time. The reserve is open from sunrise to sunset.

For a brochure giving complete details on fishing, write: Lake Katharine Nature Preserve, 784 Rock Run Road, Jackson, Ohio 45640.

LAKE LOGAN
400 Acres
Ohio 664,
two miles
southwest of Logan
in Hocking County

Anglers have good reason to believe the next state record saugeye will be caught at Lake Logan, a productive 400-acre park lake near Logan.

The current record, a 12.42-pound saugeye taken on March 29, 1993 by Daniel D'Amore of Swanton, was a Lake Logan fish. It was enticed with a twister tail near the beach.

It was a catch that returned the state record honor to Lake Logan after it was lost temporarily to a fisherman who caught a 10 1/4-pound saugeye at Wills Creek Dam.

Lake Logan was first stocked with the hybrid in 1984, and yearly since 1990. With excellent survival of the stocked fish and good growth rates, there is reason to think saugeye fishing will remain very good into the next century.

People still are talking about the unidentified angler who, in the spring of 1989, came off Lake Logan with a stringer of five saugeyes that weighed about 7-pounds apiece.

Over the years some huge bass have been taken from Lake Logan. Fishery workers are confident that Logan contains bass up to 20 to 22 inches.

Still, the lake earns only a "fair" rating in the current outlook for bass fishing. Fair also is the proper description of what can be expected from the bluegills.

Channel catfish are doing well. Besides natural reproduction, channel numbers are supplemented with stocking on alternating years. Catfish from 10 to 20 inches are plentiful.

Some 300 Christmas trees were submerged in the lake as fish attractors in 1989.

Lake Logan is in a state park with a hiking trail, picnicking areas and a swimming beach. A launching ramp is present and motors up to 10 horsepower can be used.

LAKE RUPERT
325 Acres
Ohio 93, four
miles south of
McArthur in Vinton County

Ohio doesn't have many lakes with a fishing outlook as good as the one for 325-acre Lake Rupert in 1,249-acre Wellston Wildlife Area.

The forecasts: Bass - excellent; Channel catfish - excellent; bluegill - very good; saugeye - up and coming.

To all this, fairly good crappie fishing in the spring can be added as a bonus.

"Lake Rupert is a lake where everything seems to be working for us," says Dave Bright, district fish management supervisor in southeast Ohio.

The division adopted a 12- to 15-inch slot limit on bass in 1990 to encourage the keeping of the smaller bass less than 12 inches, or the larger ones longer than 15. Meanwhile, the slot protects the bass most capable of replenishing the lake.

"The slot limit has had phenomenal

A 12- to 15-inch slot limit on bass applies at Lake Rupert.

results," says Bright, citing test netting that found bass up to 5, 6 and even 7 pounds in the reservoir.

Saugeye stocking began in 1991. Annual releases of fingerling saugeyes at a rate of 100 per acre is producing a year around fishery for the walleye-sauger hybrid. Some of the fish have grown to 25 inches at Rupert.

Anglers find plenty of spots to fish because of the fish attractors submerged in the reservoir. A map showing the placement of the attractors has been prepared by the Division of Wildlife and is available at the district office in Athens, if not at local bait and tackle stores.

Lake Rupert is frequently referred to as Wellston City Reservoir. Boat owners will find a good ramp. Motors up to 10 horsepower may be used.

LAKE SNOWDEN
150 Acres
off U.S. 50,
a half mile
northeast of Albany
in Athens County

The introduction of saugeyes at Lake Snowden in 1994 is adding another dimension to this fishing lake west of Athens.

Fishing for the hybrid should get progressively better into the 2000 years, complementing the bluegill fishing that is excellent.

Besides a goodly number of bluegills in the 6- to 8-inch range, Snowden has redear sunfish up to 9 inches.

Catfish is another target at Snowden. The lake is stocked with channels on an alternate year cycle with "cats" in the 11- to 17-inch range plentiful. It's not uncommon to pull in a 10-pound channel.

Snowden bass regulations have progressed from a 14-inch minimum size limit from 1983 to '89, to a 13- to 16-inch slot limit in 1990 and '91 and the current 12- to 15-inch slot that was started in 1992.

Fishery biologists think that the harvest of bass less than 12 inches would be beneficial to the lake by promoting the growth rate of larger bass and keeping in check the population of small panfish.

Lake Snowden is the right size for a small boat. A ramp is provided and outboard motors up to six horsepower can be used.

LAKE WHITE
323 Acres
Ohio 104, 4 miles south of
Waverly in Pike County

Lake White south of Chillicothe offers more fishing opportunity than it appears.

Although the reservoir has many private homes along the shore and a liberal, unlimited horsepower rating for a lake of only 323 acres, fish management programs have created new fishing opportunities.

The most important one is the saugeye fishing that can be enjoyed in the lake and sometimes below the spillway. The hybrid fish was introduced in 1986. Within a few years saugeyes up to 5 pounds were being taken.

In recent years, the fish has been stocked at a rate of 100 per acre. The fishing outlook for saugeyes is good through the 1990s.

Excellent catfishing has been produced through the stocking of channels on alternate years. Catfish also reproduce naturally.

Bluegills and white crappies are in the lake and the size range of both leaves a lot to be desired. Bass fishing is mediocre.

State park visitors will find a campground and picnicking area, as well as a good ramp that offers convenient access to the water.

OHIO POWER RECREATION AREA
350 lakes in 20,000 acres
Eastern Ohio

"It's a diamond in the rough," says Mike Greenlee, assistant fish management supervisor in southeast Ohio for the Ohio Division of Wildlife.

"Make that a bunch of diamonds," others might say about Ohio Power Recreation Area, an outdoor mecca in eastern Ohio that extends southward from Zanesville.

With more than 300 ponds in a rugged section of the state it's easy to understand why Ohio Power has won the respect of outdoors people. The little lakes range in size from less than an acre up to 20 acres.

A person who doesn't mind hiking could fish several of these little lakes in one day and would not encounter much, if any, fishing pressure.

Most of the ponds have bass, bluegills, other sunfish, catfish and crappies. If you have a bellyboat, this is the place to use it. Trophy bass up to seven or eight pounds might be taken from a secluded pond.

When new lakes are created they are stocked with bass, bluegills and catfish. Yearling channel catfish are stocked in the long pond near Campground C.

Ponds vary greatly in productivity. It's wise to ask around when you are in the area. Talk to bait store owners, campers and other fishermen to seek advice on which ponds to fish.

Those wishing to visit this inviting territory can obtain a free permit to fish Ohio Power, along with a map showing the location of the lakes and campsites.

"No trespassing" zones are marked on the maps to designate areas where strip-mining or reclamation is taking place. Anglers are urged to cooperate with our friends at Ohio Power Company, the land owner.

For a free, lifetime permit to fish this area, write: Ohio Power Recreation Area, P.O. Box 328, McConnelsville, Ohio 43756, or Division of Wildlife, District Four Office, 360 E. State Street, Athens, OH 45701.

See Lake map on page 114

PIEDMONT LAKE

2,270 Acres between Cambridge and Cadiz, off Ohio 800, 10 miles north of I-70 in Belmont and Harrison counties.

When Joe D. Lykins battled to his boat a 50 1/4-inch, 55-pound, 2-ounce muskellunge on April 12, 1972, no one, including Joe, thought this Ohio state record fish still would be the record 25 years later.

It is. And Piedmont is still the lake where someone, someday, has a chance of topping the mighty musky taken a quarter of a century ago by Joe Lykins.

"We have a real consistent stocking program at Piedmont and good musky fishing," says Mike Greenlee, assistant fish management supervisor.

Piedmont is not just for the musky fans, though. The 2,300-acre lake in the Muskingum Conservancy District is noted for yielding a variety of fish, including largemouth bass, smallmouth bass, bluegills, white crappies, black crappies, channel catfish and flathead catfish up to 50 pounds, and then some.

Adding to the lineup of fish now beckoning the angler is the saugeye. This fish was introduced at Piedmont in 1989 with the release of 102,000 fingerlings. About 161,000 were added in 1990.

Some of the saugeyes from the '89 release were keeper size by fall of '91, suggesting an excellent growth rate. The saugeye opportunity has been expanded through yearly plantings of fingerlings. Excellent fishing for this hybrid can be expected through the 1990s.

The 10-mile long lake built for flood-control and recreation in 1942 is one of the most scenic reservoirs in the Conservancy District. A variety of fish inhabit the water because of the food and cover available to them.

Besides rocky shorelines, points, slopes, flats and large shallow coves, anglers will find three types of aquatic vegetation: curlyleaf pondweed, coontail and milfoil.

Despite its superb fishing potential, Piedmont is not heavily fished. It is not close to a major city and the 10-horsepower limit means it is not the preferred lake of boat owners who want to run their large engines.

Facilities at the lake include two boat ramps, a campground and a fully-

Ohio musky fisherman Rudy Kimball landed this 49-inch, 27 1/4-pound musky at Piedmont Lake on six-pound line.

77

equipped marina with rental boats, bait and tackle.

See Lake map on page 122

SALT FORK LAKE
2,952 Acres off Ohio 22, 8 miles northeast of Cambridge, in Guernsey County

Invite a friend to go fishing at Salt Fork Lake near Cambridge and chances are he, or she, will want to join you. If not, your friend hasn't kept up with the fishing.

Salt Fork is one of Ohio's top all-around fishing lakes. You want crappies? Salt Fork has them. Walleyes? Is a 10- to 12-pound walleye big enough? Bass? Salt Fork is where the tournament fishermen like to go.

Both largemouth and smallmouth bass can be found in Salt Fork Lake. A 15-inch minimum size limit on bass, in place since 1992, has improved the fishing.

Salt Fork also has the reputation as one of the top lakes in the state for the sharp-tooth, battling muskellunge.

In fact, long and narrow Salt Fork, spreading through the hills of Guernsey County, is an inviting place for the pleasure boater and water skier, as well as the angler. Fortunately, there are many bays, and no wake zones where an angler can find quiet water.

Crappies provide most of the fishing action in the spring. Finding these fish has been made easier because of the 3,320 Christmas trees set out as fish attractors in 1990, '91, '95 and 1,000 more in 1997. Salt Fork has white and black crappies.

Salt Fork Lake, with good fishing, plus cabins, golf and a lodge, is an appealing place for a family vacation.

Walleyes are doing fine. Biologists say that some of the older ones weigh 10 to 12 pounds.

Stocking of walleye began with the planting of 720,000 walleye fry in 1987, followed by 200,000 fingerlings in 1988, 89,000 fingerlings in '89 and 131,000 in '90.

Walleye stocking continues on a yearly basis with the release of 100 fingerlings per acre.

Salt Fork is a high priority lake for muskellunge stocking because the lake produces for anglers. The vicinity of the dam is one of the favorite areas to troll for muskies during summer months.

Other fish at Salt Fork include channel catfish up to 15 pounds. Bluegills are plentiful in the 5 1/2- to 7-inch range and redears are increasing in numbers.

An all-purpose area, Salt Fork State Park offers recreation for the entire family. That includes a lodge, cabins, campground, beach, golf course, good boat ramps and a full-service marina.

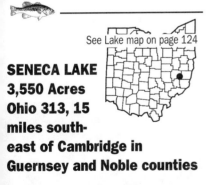

See Lake map on page 124

SENECA LAKE
3,550 Acres
Ohio 313, 15
miles south-
east of Cambridge in
Guernsey and Noble counties

Seneca Lake is the only lake in Ohio stocked with striped bass, and for two reasons. The largest lake in the Muskingum Conservancy District is a good choice for the super sport fish and

it is close to the state fish hatchery where hybrid striped bass are produced.

The hybrid, a cross between a white bass and a striped bass, has become a favorite species at several lakes around the state. So besides affording a target for anglers at Seneca, the striper serves as brood stock for the stocking program.

Stripers up to 35 inches have been caught at Seneca. One must pull in at least a 26-incher to have a keeper. The creel limit is one.

Most people who fish Seneca think bass. The lake has plenty of 14- to 16-inch bass with some running up to 20 inches, if not longer.

The island at Seneca is an excellent area to fish for bass, as are the deeper coves with woody cover. Seneca has a 15-inch minimum size limit for bass.

Though once regarded as a great crappie lake, Seneca no longer enjoys that reputation. Besides the bass and the possibility of hooking a big striper, Seneca's prime targets have become the catfish and walleye.

Catfish are abundant with some of the channels approaching state-record size. Perhaps Seneca will surpass the record now held by a 37-pound, 10.4-ounce fish taken at LaDue Reservoir in 1992.

Walleye fingerlings are stocked yearly since 1990. Anglers who have learned the location of the humps in the lake and fish them through the summer have done well. Walleyes up to 30 inches have been seen.

In February and March of 1996, about 600 Christmas trees were set out as fish attractors. A similar project took place three years earlier.

Besides channel cats, flathead catfish

up to 50 pounds are said to be in Seneca Lake. Bluegills are plentiful and some run up to 8 inches, if you can find them.

Seneca is one of the most developed Conservancy areas with good launching ramps, well supplied marinas, campgrounds and housekeeping cabins.

Here's another thing about Seneca. It's probably the only inland lake in Ohio with a 180 horsepower limit on motors.

TYCOON LAKE
204 Acres on
Ohio 554
northeast of Rio Grande in
Gallia County

Find out where the fisheries biologist goes fishing and chances are you have discovered a good place to fish.

In southeast Ohio, it's no secret. "My favorite place is Tycoon Lake," says Mike Greenlee, assistant fish management supervisor.

Dave Bright, fish management supervisor, also likes Tycoon. "We've had phenomenal results with the 15-inch minimum size limit on bass since 1995," Bright stated.

The biologists say the 204-acre lake yields several 8-pound bass a year, a number of bass larger than 15 inches and excellent catch-and-release fishing for bass shorter than 15 inches.

Still, bass is not the main reason Greenlee likes Tycoon. "I go there for the bluegills. It's not like it used to be when you could catch bluegills 9 and 10 inches, but it's still pretty good," Greenlee said.

The biologists believe that Tycoon's reputation for monster bluegills may have caused too much fishing pressure on the panfish. Moreover, small bluegills escape predator fish in aquatic vegetation.

Grass carp were released in the fall of 1996 with the idea of reducing the vegetation. That could make more food available to bass and reduce the number of small bluegills.

Tycoon lies in a 480-acre wildlife area that will appeal to the angler who likes a small, quiet, get-away-from-it-all lake.

A project at Tycoon that may have improved fishing is one that added nutrients to the water. In 1988, 17 wooden pallets were submerged in the lake. Each was to gradually emit a phosphate fertilizer. The project has been completed, but researchers have not published their findings.

Tycoon has a fair number of decent-size crappies, plus warmouth bass and redear sunfish.

Channel catfish have been stocked since 1983 and are doing well. Channels up to 28 pounds have been caught.

Fishing is from the bank or a small boat. A boat ramp is provided and electric trolling motors may be used.

Put on a worm, toss it in, Tycoon Lake fish are ready.

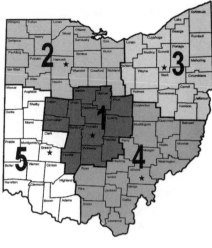

Cameron Tenhover knows how to catch the hybrid striped bass at East Fork Lake.

District 5, Lakes in Southwest Ohio

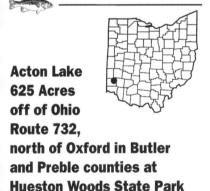

Acton Lake 625 Acres off of Ohio Route 732, north of Oxford in Butler and Preble counties at Hueston Woods State Park

More than a year ago, biologists from District 5 of the Ohio Division of Wildlife conducted an electrofishing study on Acton Lake. They were checking to see if a 15-inch minimum size limit imposed on largemouth bass was working, raising the average size of that species in this small lake close to the Indiana line.

Out went the electric shocks and up came the bass, plenty of them. And with the size showing improvement, Action Lake is already a healthy habitat for bass and it should get better.

"We are pleased with the results of the 15-inch size limit at Acton Lake," said Doug Maloney, district fish management supervisor. "It appears as if there are more bass in the lake, both larger and smaller than 15 inches. Many fishermen have noticed that and their results seem to be agreeing with our surveys."

Acton lake is just one part of one of the best state-owned recreation complexes in southwest Ohio. Hueston Woods State Park is a full-service facility, with a lodge, cabins, nature center, hiking and horseback riding trails, marina, campground and beach.

Crappie fishing has bounced back from a large kill in the late 1980s and it's always been a good lake for bluegills and catfish.

A maximum 10 horsepower limit keeps the lake calm and, for the most part, quiet. Perhaps the loudest noise you'll hear is from the resident giant Canada geese as they cross the lake.

Adams Lake
47 Acres
near West
Union on Ohio Route 41
in Adams County

Perhaps not many anglers have heard about this very small southern Ohio Lake. Perhaps one reason is the fishing isn't very good.

The fact is, Adams Lake is a rebuilding project. The lake was drained in the early 1990s when the Division of Parks and Recreation replaced the dam. It was then stocked with largemouth bass, bluegills and channel catfish.

Although the lake is beginning to come back, the fish haven't had much time to grow, so bluegills and catfish are small. Bass are so small, it would be rare to catch one over the 15-inch minimum size limit, so for now it is a catch-and-release lake for bass. And since it is so small, electric motors only are allowed.

Anglers enjoy a quiet day at Grant Lake, another small reservoir in southwest Ohio.

See Lake map on page 98

C.J. Brown
Reservoir
2,120 Acres
on Route 4 in Clark County,
a mile north of Springfield

If it weren't for Lake Erie, C.J. Brown Reservoir might easily be called the walleye capital of Ohio. It is, at least, the best place to catch walleyes in the southwest part of the state.

Stocked annually by the Ohio Division of Wildlife with about 212,000 walleye fingerlings, C.J. Brown has been one of the state's real success stories for its stocking program. Because of the lake's ability to grow large walleyes, eggs and sperm are often collected from the lake and taken to hatcheries to supply this and other Ohio lakes with fingerlings.

Walleyes are generally found near the dam in about 20 feet of water in the spring. Most successful anglers use a jig or a light-colored twister tail, sometimes tipped with a minnow. Later, walleyes move toward the middle of the lake, the areas often referred to as the old roadbeds or the "humps." A quick trip around the area with a depth finder will show you what is meant by "humps."

Most of the summer walleyes are caught trolling. Planer boards can be effective, since walleyes are often suspended. It's best to watch the fish finder and troll at various depths. Bottom bouncers are effective, but so is the weight-forward spinner tipped with a nightcrawler in the warmer weather.

There is a minimum size limit on

walleyes of 15 inches. Sometimes it is late in the season before large numbers are fattened up enough to be keepers. The limit seems to be working to create a fishery with larger walleyes. An 11-pounder was taken there a couple of years ago.

Biologists feel C.J. Brown is a good walleye lake because not many are lost through the dam. Although they likely do not reproduce on their own, the habitat is good enough to insure a high survival rate for those stocked.

C.J. Brown doesn't have a great deal of cover and there is only one boat ramp, although it's a wide one. The water can be rough, not just from wind, but from the large number of pleasure craft using the lake, especially on summer weekends. The lake is patrolled by the Ohio Division of Watercraft and rangers from Buck Creek State Park, but it can get crowded at peak skiing and personal watercraft times. The best bet is to fish on weekdays or early in the morning on weekends.

While the lake is not blessed with great cover, it does contain a fairly large population of crappies. The best place to fish for crappies is between the boat launching ramp, the marina and around pilings placed in the lake for cover. There are also sunken Christmas trees there to provide habitat for crappies and bluegills. Traditional baits, like minnows and waxworms, are effective all year and there are bait shops in the area as you approach the lake.

C.J. Brown does not have a great reputation as a bass lake, but at certain times of the year it turns on. For largemouth bass, your best bet is to work the shoreline on the north end of the lake with plastic worms, spinners and crankbaits. Try the riprap around the dam in the fall.

There are also plenty of channel catfish and the white bass population seems to get bigger each year. So far, the white bass haven't harmed the walleye population. When trolling for walleyes in the summer, it's not uncommon to pick up a white bass, channel cat or even a large crappie.

Camping is available at Buck Creek State Park along with cabins and a large beach.

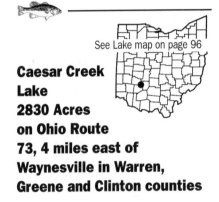

See Lake map on page 96

Caesar Creek Lake
2830 Acres on Ohio Route 73, 4 miles east of Waynesville in Warren, Greene and Clinton counties

If you are looking for a getaway at one of the most scenic spots in southwest Ohio, consider spending some time at Caesar Creek Lake.

There are plenty of things to do for an entire family. The large campground offers Rent-A-Camps and Rent-An-RV. There's a beach and although there is no marina, one is in the future plans.

Caesar Creek is a large, deep lake with several boat ramps. It is owned by the Army Corps of Engineers and used as part of the Ohio River flood control system. Although the water levels can be raised or lowered, there is usually access all year. In addition to the Corps of Engineers, the Ohio divisions of parks and wildlife have jurisdiction over different areas.

The state park offers a large beach, miles of hiking trails and bridle trails, including a horseman's camp. A nature center also presents regular programs and offers hikes around the picturesque lake. A particularly good time to visit is in the fall when some of the colors are spectacular.

While Caesar Creek has many species of fish, the saugeye is the newest attraction. Although you will find saugeyes all over the lake, the most popular spot seems to be the flats near Walker Island. Early you will have good luck with minnows on twistertails, but you might switch to weight-forward spinners tipped with nightcrawlers later in the year. You might also try fishing the tailwaters of the dam for saugeyes, especially after a rain.

A few walleyes can be found in Caesar Creek Lake, but they haven't been stocked since 1991. Saugeyes have simply been a more hearty fish there.

Some large crappies were taken from the lake in the early 1990s. The best spots for crappies and bluegills are in the coves and around the stickups. There is a large amount of cover on the north side of the lake where Caesar Creek enters. If you put in at the Haines Road boat ramp, you are right there. Minnows, jigs and waxworms are the appropriate baits all year.

Some of the lake's best fishing takes place during the white bass runs, usually in April and May. Watch for spawning in the creeks then later you're likely find white bass in the areas around the Route 73 bridge and Walker Island.

Caesar Creek Lake also holds a large number of channel catfish, ranging in size up to 14 pounds. There are also some flathead catfish caught every year, some more than 20 pounds.

Largemouth bass do well early in the spring and late in the fall. Fish along the banks on the south side of the lake early in the morning or around sunset. A tip from Doug Maloney, district fish management supervisor: Use your fishfinder and look for humps and drop-offs in

"I go for catfish and catch bass; I go for bass and catch musky," says Randy Kempton, Chillicothe, fishing Tri-River Bass Club Early Bird Tournament at Rocky Fork Lake.

depths of 15-feet or less, even if it's away from shore. Those spots generally get little or no pressure.

Since Caesar Creek is the only lake of any size close to Dayton, there is plenty of action there, especially on summer weekends and holidays. Although there are areas of the lake pleasure boats and personal watercraft cannot go, especially in the creeks and around stickups, it can be a very busy place. It's best to pick your fishing times with that in mind, since most of the main boat ramps will be crowded when the water skiers and other speedboats are out. There is also a handicapped-access fishing dock near the dam.

Clark Lake 110 Acres East of Springfield off of Old U.S. 40 in Clark County

In the spring, you can count on some 5-7-pound largemouth bass being caught. There are large numbers of small bass, but there is some quality.

This small lake near Springfield also has been producing some nice white crappies in recent years, many in the 10-12-inch size. It's rated just fair for bluegills with most being small. There are also a good number of small bullheads.

While the fish generally are not large, it's a good lake to take small children, because there is a decent amount of shore fishing access, including three piers. It's a peaceful lake, mainly

because of the electric-motors-only restriction.

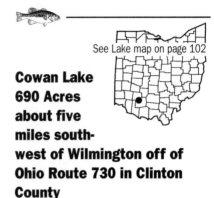

See Lake map on page 102

Cowan Lake 690 Acres about five miles southwest of Wilmington off of Ohio Route 730 in Clinton County

Picture yourself casting for bass along the banks of Cowan Lake. Many people do.

Then, all of a sudden, Wham! A fish hits, but that's no bass!

It's a musky!!

Musky fishing has improved at Cowan Lake in recent years. That, along with an unexplained decline in musky success at nearby Rocky Fork Lake has made Cowan the best musky lake in southwest Ohio.

If you want a tip on musky fishing at Cowan, look up Calvin Pyle at South Shore Marina and he'll pass along tips on Musky fishing, Pyle-Style.

Chances are, you are going to do well with bass at Cowan Lake, too. It might be the best bass lake in the area, with lots of cover.

Jim Corbin of Yellow Springs says Cowan is a great lake for fly fishing. He does it every chance he gets. Not only do bass hit his flies, but he says it's great fun fly fishing for bluegills.

Like most places, crappie fishing is off and on at Cowan, but when it's on it's usually very good. White bass turn on at various times of the year.

A growing numbers of anglers visit Cowan just to go after the channel catfish. Some up to 20 pounds have been taken. Try the muddy areas where the creeks come in.

Cowan Lake State Park has a campground, cabins and two beaches. There is a 10 horsepower limit on the lake.

East Fork Lake
2,160 Acres off Ohio Route 222, four miles southeast of Batavia in Clermont County

The name of the game at East Fork is hybrid striped bass. One of the few lakes stocked with the hybrid stripers, it has been an outstanding lake for the hard-fighting cross between a striper and a white bass for several years.

The Division of Wildlife began stocking the hybrids in 1983. Each year a million hybrid striper fry are stocked there and now fish weighing up to 14 pounds are being taken. A 15-inch size limit helped improve the size of East Fork hybrids and a four-fish bag limit helps keep the numbers up.

Live shad and shad-like lures are usually the best bets for catching stripers. Try casting a shiny lure into a swelling of shad. Those eating machine stripers are bound to be nearby.

While the striped bass seem to get most of the publicity, fishing for other species is also very good. Fishing for bass - largemouth, smallmouth and spotted - usually is excellent. Crappie fishing has been very good in recent years.

Large numbers and sizes of channel catfish are present. Some range up to 26 inches and 10 pounds.

Located near Cincinnati, East Fork gets a large amount of boat traffic on weekends. If you can choose your time, it's best to fish there on week days or early in the morning on weekends. There is a campground, beach and nearby bait and tackle shops.

See Lake map on page 106

Grand Lake St. Marys
Ohio 703
13,500 Acres in Mercer and Auglaize counties, between Celina and St. Marys

You've probably heard about Grand Lake St. Marys for its outstanding crappie fishing. It has earned that reputation over the years. But the big news at Grand Lake isn't crappies, it's yellow perch.

That great crappie lake is also a great perch lake with perhaps the best Ohio perch fishing this side of Lake Erie. One comical local angler even pointed out that because of recent perch population problems in Lake Erie, the Division of Wildlife might consider stocking it from Grand Lake St. Marys.

It's good, but not that good.

Perch have always been in Grand Lake, but they were scarce and small. A few years ago, they started showing up in decent numbers during ice fishing season. And some were even considered jumbo, at 10-11 inches.

The trend has continued all year. Late summer and early fall are probably the best times to catch ringed perch at Grand Lake, but they can be caught at other times if you work for them. And ice fishing for them remains very productive.

Biologists can't say for sure why yellow perch are suddenly so prolific at Grand Lake St. Marys, except that the water quality has improved because of a completed sewer system on the south side of the lake and the gizzard shad population has been high.

St. Marys is one of the few lakes in Ohio that is not stocked by the state. There are plenty of fish there and they seem to reproduce with little trouble. In addition to crappies and yellow perch, there are also plenty of largemouth bass, channel catfish, bullheads, bluegills and, of course, carp. You'll also find an occasional northern pike (although there probably aren't enough to fish for them) and even a possible large striper (once stocked, one or two a season are still caught in early spring).

Although the lake is very popular with all kinds of boaters, it is large enough to accommodate all water enthusiasts. The south side has a large designated no-wake zone, which provides the best fishing. In addition there are numerous channels on that side of the lake, which provide good fishing cover even on windy days. If the lake level is down, be sure to watch out for propeller-eating stumps. It's best to watch the channel markers.

Grand Lake St. Marys is the largest inland lake in Ohio. It has a state park with a campground and beach and there are several marinas around the lake. There are even a few restaurants where you can dock your boat and stop for a meal.

State facilities on both the east and west ends of the lake offer easy access for boaters and plenty of riprap for bank fishermen. The east bank has parking areas almost up to the water, so non-boaters can bring a lunch and lawn chairs and fish all day. That, by the way, is a good place to land big catfish, especially on summer evenings. There is also

Grand Lake St. Marys yields an abundant supply of catfish along with superb fishing for crappies and yellow perch.

a handicapped-access fishing dock on the east side.

Traditionally, a good spot for crappies has been the Windy Point area near Montezuma on the lake's southwest side.

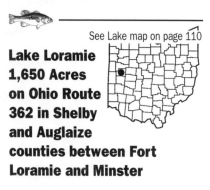

See Lake map on page 110

Lake Loramie 1,650 Acres on Ohio Route 362 in Shelby and Auglaize counties between Fort Loramie and Minster

The buzz at Lake Loramie is not about fish you can catch now, but about future fishing in this Western Ohio lake.

The state started a stocking program for saugeyes in 1996. If they do well and continue to be stocked, the lake could turn into another saugeye super lake in a few years, much the same as nearby Indian Lake. The saugeye has put the Indian Lake region back on the map, so to speak, and local leaders are hoping for the same for Lake Loramie.

Although not a large lake, Loramie is a good fishing lake for several reasons. For one there are large no-wake zones, which keep down pleasure boating. Another good reason is the number of channels with access for bank fishermen. The state park provides several spots with parking, picnic tables and restrooms for anglers.

While most people fish for largemouth bass from boats, it's very possible to pick up a largemouth while casting from a bank into one of the chan-

Mark Sisco uses throw net to catch shad at East Fork Lake, and shad takes this hybrid striped bass.

Glorious day of fishing at Rocky Fork Lake ends with a picturesque sunset.

nels. Of course those same spots produce numerous bluegills, crappies, carp and channel cats. And you can always catch bullheads at Lake Loramie.

"Bullheads are tremendous at Lake Loramie," said Doug Maloney, district fish management supervisor for the Ohio Division of Wildlife. "March and April are the best times for bullheads."

The state park campground is picturesque with many sites right along the water. There are marinas and bait shops in several spots around the lake.

Paint Creek Lake
1,190 Acres
on U.S. 50, 17
miles east of
Hillsboro in Highland and
Ross counties

See Lake map on page 112

Paint Creek Lake is many different lakes in one. It all depends on the weather.

After prolonged periods of rain, the lake's large watershed can bring the water level up quickly at this flood-control lake. Since the main reason for the lake in the first place is to protect the Ohio River area, the Army Corps is often obligated to keep the water level high in Paint Creek and other lakes to avoid massive flooding downstream.

In recent years, spring seasons have been extremely wet and Paint Creek has flooded to the extent of making many of the state park facilities, including boat ramps unusable. Sometimes it takes weeks for the water levels to drop far enough to bring the lake back to its full fishing potential.

When all is well, Paint Creek Lake is very good for bass, crappie and saugeye fishing. Saugeyes have been stocked heavily, at about 600,000 per year and it's paying off with bigger and better catches each year. The state has been studying the consequences when large quantities of water pass through the dam. The discharge might be taking large numbers of saugeyes with it, cutting the lake's saugeye population. But so far, anglers are still catching them.

One of the most popular places for anglers to catch saugeyes has been in the tailwaters below the dam. There are plenty of places to fish from the bank in that area and some of the biggest saugeyes are often caught there. And not only is it a good spring fishery, but many local anglers give the tailwaters a workout throughout the winter as long as there's water flowing through the dam.

There is a good population of channel catfish with many in the 12-16 inch range. Some flatheads up to 20 pounds are landed each year.

Like Caesar Creek, Paint Creek provides a very picturesque setting for fall anglers with lots of colorful trees in and around the many bays.

See Lake map on page 120

Rocky Fork Lake
2,080 Acres
on Ohio Route 124, east of
Hillsboro in Highland County

Fishing at this popular southwest Ohio lake seems to run in cycles. For example, crappies were small in size and numbers for a few years in the early 1990s, but began to bounce back toward the middle of the decade.

Rocky Fork used to be a good lake for muskies, stocked annually by the state, but they became hard to come by in the mid-90s.

Once wildlife officials figure out what has been happening with muskies there, they'll probably bounce back, too.

In the meantime, there are some constants at Rocky Fork Lake. Walleyes have been coming on there in recent years with the state stocking about 225,000 each year. They're caught by various methods at different times of the year, some even by bass fishermen tossing lures close to the banks, but most by traditional walleye methods like casting or trolling weight-forward spinners tipped with nightcrawlers.

Speaking of bass, Rocky Fork is one of those lakes that seems to support both largemouth and smallmouth, although the former is more prevalent. It's usually considered a good lake for bass tournaments and several area clubs gather at Rocky Fork each year.

Some flathead catfish over 30 pounds have been brought in, along with good numbers of channel catfish up to 15 inches. Night fishing is usually most productive.

With crappies coming back, Rocky Fork resumes its former reputation as a good panfish lake. There have always been plenty of bluegills, so it's a good place to take kids fishing. The state park on the west end of the lake has a camp-

Tresa Northrup, Xenia, fishes at Rocky Fork Lake.

ground and docks, but some of the best fishing spots are along the north shore and around the dam on the southeast corner.

Rush Run Lake
50 Acres
off of Ohio Route 725 in
Preble County

Bluegills. Big bluegills and plenty of them. If you can't catch a bluegill at Rush Run, it's likely you just can't catch a fish, anywhere.

The lake is filled with them and they probably have the best average size of any lake in southwest Ohio. It might be the best place around to take children to fish and just about guarantee they'll catch one.

Bass fishing is good, but not great. A slot limit (12-15 inches) was tried to raise the size of largemouth in the lake, but was recently dropped, since many small bass still exist. You can, however, pull in some big bass from Rush Run, especially in the spring, with some over 5 pounds. Now there's a 15-inch minimum size limit.

You'll also find some crappies, but not many.

You can bring your bass boat, but don't plan on getting your propeller wet. Electric motors only is the law.

Scioto Brush Creek is one of many outstanding rivers to fish in southwestern Ohio.

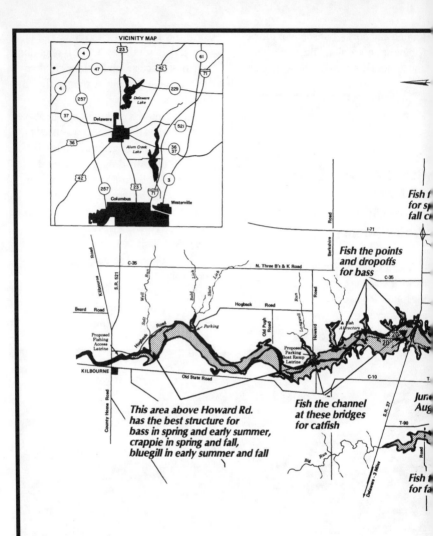

VICINITY MAP

4 · 23

47 · 61

42 · 71

4 · 229

257 · Delaware Lake

37 · Delaware · 521

36 · Alum Creek Lake · 36 37

42 · 3

257 · 23 71

Columbus · Westerville

Fish f
for s
fall c

Road

I-71

Berkshire Road

**Fish the points
and dropoffs
for bass**

C-35

N. Three B's & K Road

Kilbourne Road

S.R. 521

C-35

Salt Run

Bald Lick

Slate Lick

Hogback Road

Longwell Run

Howard Road

Beard Road

Hogback Road

Parking

Old Pugh Road

▲ Fish Attractors

20

Proposed
Fishing
Access
Latrine

Proposed
Parking
Boat Ramp
Latrine

KILBOURNE

Old State Road

C-10

T-

County Home Road

**This area above Howard Rd.
has the best structure for
bass in spring and early summer,
crappie in spring and fall,
bluegill in early summer and fall**

**Fish the channel
at these bridges
for catfish**

S.R. 37

Jun
Aug

T-90

Big Run

Delaware - 3 Miles

Road

Fish
for fa

Fishing spots

marked by Division of
Wildlife fishing experts

92

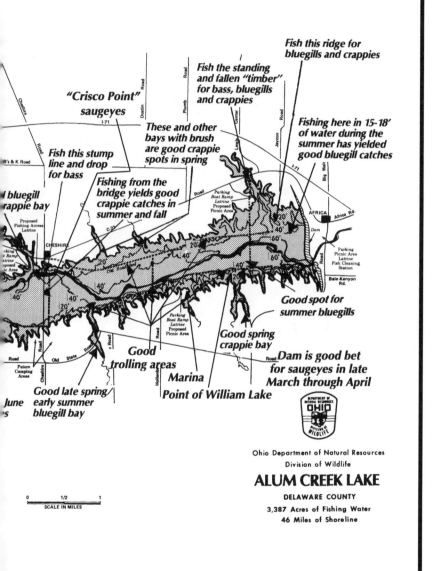

Fish this ridge for bluegills and crappies

Fish the standing and fallen "timber" for bass, bluegills and crappies

"Crisco Point" saugeyes

Fishing here in 15-18' of water during the summer has yielded good bluegill catches

These and other bays with brush are good crappie spots in spring

Fish this stump line and drop for bass

bluegill rappie bay

Fishing from the bridge yields good crappie catches in summer and fall

AFRICA

Africa Rd.

Parking
Boat Ramp
Latrine
Proposed
Picnic Area

Parking
Picnic Area
Latrine
Fish Cleaning
Station

CHESHIRE

Bale-Kenyon Rd.

Good spot for summer bluegills

Parking
Boat Ramp
Latrine
Proposed
Picnic Area

Good spring crappie bay

Dam is good bet for saugeyes in late March through April

Good trolling areas

Marina

Point of William Lake

Future Camping Areas

Good late spring/ early summer bluegill bay

June

Ohio Department of Natural Resources
Division of Wildlife

ALUM CREEK LAKE

DELAWARE COUNTY
3,387 Acres of Fishing Water
46 Miles of Shoreline

0   1/2   1
SCALE IN MILES

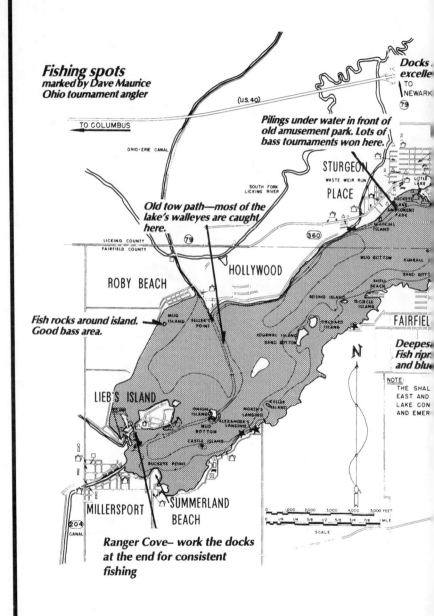

Fishing spots
marked by Dave Maurice
Ohio tournament angler

Pilings under water in front of
old amusement park. Lots of
bass tournaments won here.

Old tow path—most of the
lake's walleyes are caught
here.

Fish rocks around island.
Good bass area.

Docks
excelle
TO
NEWARK

Deepes
Fish ripr.
and blue

Ranger Cove— work the docks
at the end for consistent
fishing

94

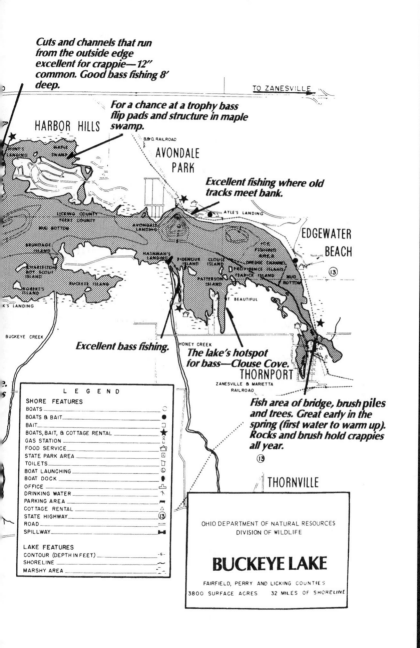

Cuts and channels that run from the outside edge excellent for crappie—12" common. Good bass fishing 8' deep.

TO ZANESVILLE

For a chance at a trophy bass flip pads and structure in maple swamp.

HARBOR HILLS

B&O. RAILROAD

AVONDALE PARK

Excellent fishing where old tracks meet bank.

HUNT'S LANDING

MAPLE SWAMP

LICKING COUNTY
PERRY COUNTY

AVONDALE LANDING

AYLE'S LANDING

EDGEWATER BEACH

MUD BOTTOM

BOUNDLEE ISLAND

ICE FISHING AREA

(13)

CHARLESTON BOY SCOUT ISLAND

HASSMAN'S LANDING

PICKNECUE ISLAND

CLOUSE ISLAND

DREDGE CHANNEL

PROVIDENCE ISLAND

MUD BOTTOM

BODREY'S ISLAND

BUCKEYE ISLAND

PATTERSON ISLAND

PROVIDENCE ISLAND

K'S LANDING

PT. BEAUTIFUL

BUCKEYE CREEK

Excellent bass fishing.

HONEY CREEK

The lake's hotspot for bass—Clouse Cove.

THORNPORT

ZANESVILLE & MARIETTA RAILROAD

Fish area of bridge, brush piles and trees. Great early in the spring (first water to warm up). Rocks and brush hold crappies all year.

(13)

THORNVILLE

OHIO DEPARTMENT OF NATURAL RESOURCES
DIVISION OF WILDLIFE

BUCKEYE LAKE

FAIRFIELD, PERRY AND LICKING COUNTIES
3800 SURFACE ACRES   32 MILES OF SHORELINE

95

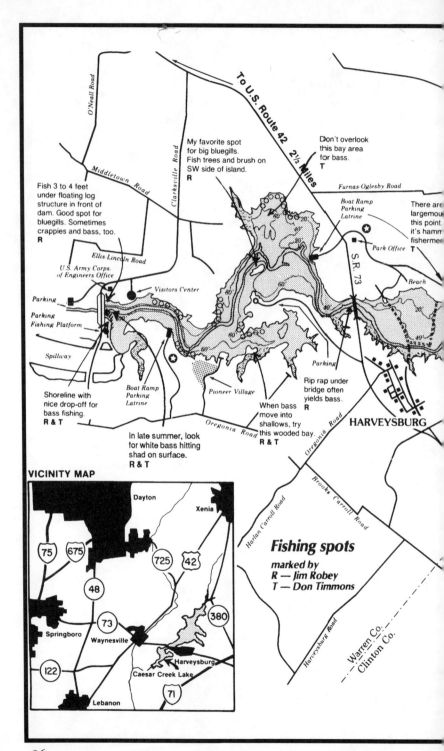

To U.S. Route 42 2½ Miles

O'Neall Road

Middletown Road

Clarksville Road

My favorite spot for big bluegills. Fish trees and brush on SW side of island.
R

Don't overlook this bay area for bass.
T

Furnas-Oglesby Road

Fish 3 to 4 feet under floating log structure in front of dam. Good spot for bluegills. Sometimes crappies and bass, too.
R

Boat Ramp
Parking
Latrine

There are largemou... this point. it's hamm... fishermen
T

Ellis-Lincoln Road

Park Office

S.R. 73

U.S. Army Corps. of Engineers Office

Visitors Center

Beach

Parking

Parking
Fishing Platform

Spillway

Shoreline with nice drop-off for bass fishing.
R & T

Boat Ramp
Parking
Latrine

Pioneer Village

Parking

Rip rap under bridge often yields bass.
R

HARVEYSBURG

When bass move into shallows, try this wooded bay.
R & T

In late summer, look for white bass hitting shad on surface.
R & T

Oregonia Road

Oregonia Road

Harlan Carroll Road

Brooks Carroll Road

VICINITY MAP

Dayton

Xenia

75   675

725   42

48

73

380

Springboro

Waynesville

122

Harveysburg

Caesar Creek Lake

Lebanon

71

Fishing spots
marked by
R — Jim Robey
T — Don Timmons

Harveysburg Road

Warren Co.
Clinton Co.

96

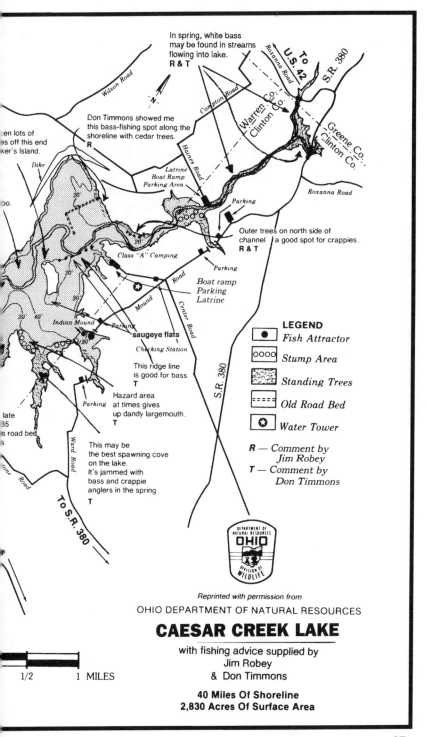

In spring, white bass may be found in streams flowing into lake. **R & T**

Don Timmons showed me this bass-fishing spot along the shoreline with cedar trees. **R**

en lots of es off this end ker's Island.

Dike

oo.

Latrine
Boat Ramp
Parking Area

Parking

Outer trees on north side of channel a good spot for crappies. **R & T**

Class "A" Camping

Parking

Boat ramp
Parking
Latrine

Indian Mound

Parking

saugeye flats

Checking Station

This ridge line is good for bass.

Hazard area at times gives up dandy largemouth. **T**

Parking

late 35 s road bed s

This may be the best spawning cove on the lake. It's jammed with bass and crappie anglers in the spring. **T**

Wilson Road

Compton Road

Haines Road

Roxanna Road

To U.S. 42
S.R. 380

Warren Co.
Clinton Co.

Greene Co.
Clinton Co.

Roxanna Road

Mound Road

Center Road

S.R. 380

Ward Road

To S.R. 380

LEGEND

● *Fish Attractor*

oooo *Stump Area*

░░░ *Standing Trees*

----- *Old Road Bed*

✪ *Water Tower*

R — *Comment by Jim Robey*

T — *Comment by Don Timmons*

DEPARTMENT OF NATURAL RESOURCES
OHIO
DIVISION OF WILDLIFE

Reprinted with permission from

OHIO DEPARTMENT OF NATURAL RESOURCES

CAESAR CREEK LAKE

with fishing advice supplied by
Jim Robey
& Don Timmons

40 Miles Of Shoreline
2,830 Acres Of Surface Area

1/2   1 MILES

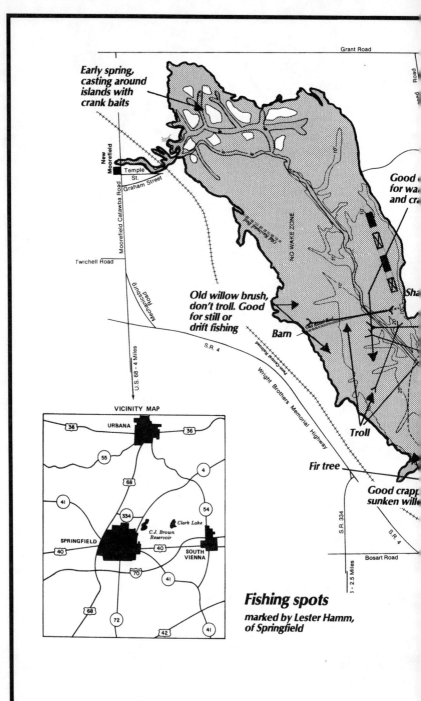

Early spring, casting around islands with crank baits

Good ...
for wa...
and cr...

Old willow brush, don't troll. Good for still or drift fishing

Barn

Sha...

Troll

Fir tree

Good crapp...
sunken will...

Grant Road

Road

New Moorefield

Temple St.

Graham Street

Moorefield Catawba Road

Twichell Road

Mechanicsburg Road

S.R. 4

U.S. 68 - 4 Miles

NO WAKE ZONE

Wright Brothers Memorial Highway

S.R. 334

S.R. 4

Bosart Road

3 - 2.5 Miles

VICINITY MAP

URBANA

36

36

55

68

4

41

54

334

Clark Lake

C.J. Brown Reservoir

SPRINGFIELD

40

40

SOUTH VIENNA

70

41

68

72

42

41

Fishing spots

marked by Lester Hamm, of Springfield

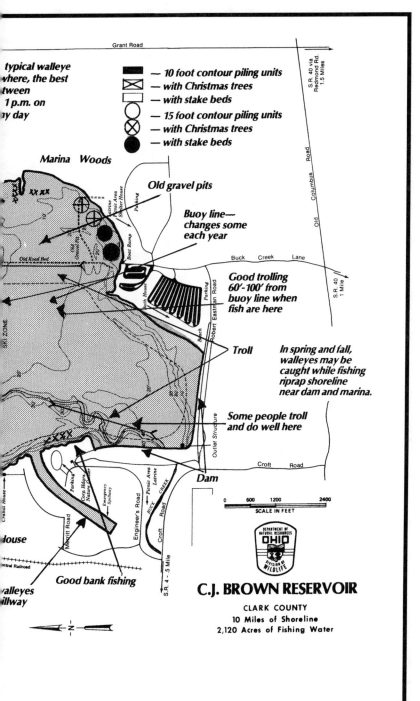

Grant Road

— 10 foot contour piling units
— with Christmas trees
— with stake beds

— 15 foot contour piling units
— with Christmas trees
— with stake beds

*typical walleye
where, the best
tween
1 p.m. on
y day*

Marina Woods

S.R. 40 via Redmond Rd. 1.5 Miles

Old Columbus Road

Old gravel pits

**Buoy line—
changes some
each year**

Buck Creek Lane

**Good trolling
60'-100' from
buoy line when
fish are here**

S.R. 40 / 1 Mile

SKI ZONE

Old Road Bed

Troll

*In spring and fall,
walleyes may be
caught while fishing
riprap shoreline
near dam and marina.*

**Some people troll
and do well here**

Croft Road

Dam

0   600   1200   2400
SCALE IN FEET

DEPARTMENT OF NATURAL RESOURCES
OHIO
DIVISION OF WILDLIFE

C.J. BROWN RESERVOIR

CLARK COUNTY
10 Miles of Shoreline
2,120 Acres of Fishing Water

ouse

*valleys
illway*

Good bank fishing

N

Latrine Picnic Area Shelter House
Parking
Boat Ramp
Bath House
Parking
Robert Eastman Road
Beach
Outlet Structure

Parking
Corp. Hdqrs. Nature Center
Emergency Spillway
Engineer's Road
Buck Picnic Area Latrine
Croft Road
Creek
Merritt Road
S.R. 4 - 5 Mile

99

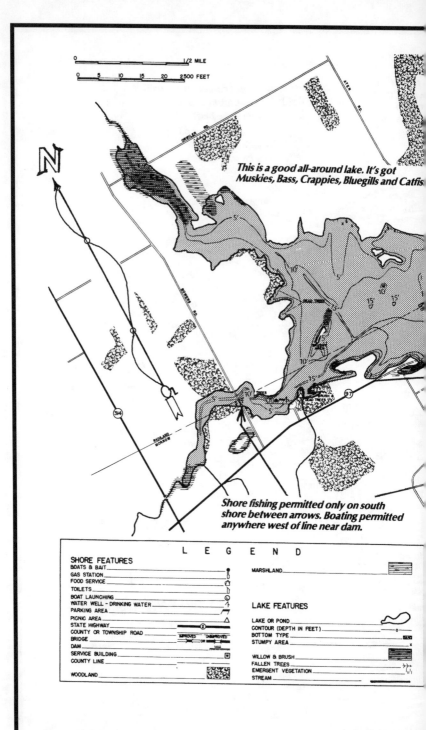

This is a good all-around lake. It's got Muskies, Bass, Crappies, Bluegills and Catfis

Shore fishing permitted only on south shore between arrows. Boating permitted anywhere west of line near dam.

L E G E N D

SHORE FEATURES
BOATS & BAIT
GAS STATION
FOOD SERVICE
TOILETS
BOAT LAUNCHING
WATER WELL - DRINKING WATER
PARKING AREA
PICNIC AREA
STATE HIGHWAY
COUNTY OR TOWNSHIP ROAD — IMPROVED UNIMPROVED
BRIDGE — OR
DAM
SERVICE BUILDING
COUNTY LINE

WOODLAND

MARSHLAND

LAKE FEATURES

LAKE OR POND
CONTOUR (DEPTH IN FEET)
BOTTOM TYPE
STUMPY AREA

WILLOW & BRUSH
FALLEN TREES
EMERGENT VEGETATION
STREAM

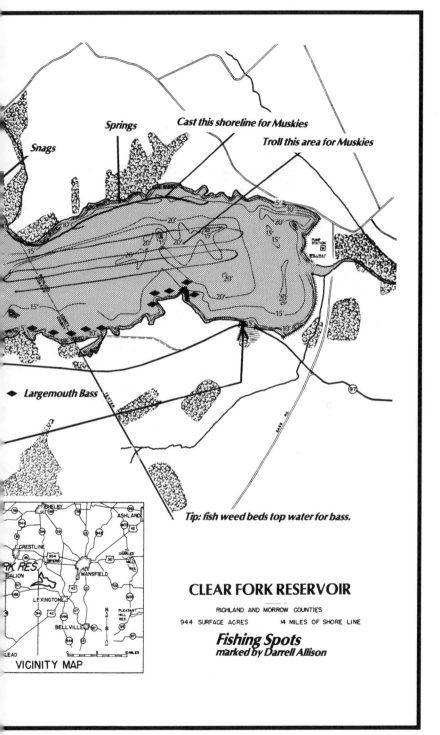

Snags

Springs

Cast this shoreline for Muskies

Troll this area for Muskies

Largemouth Bass

Tip: fish weed beds top water for bass.

CLEAR FORK RESERVOIR

RICHLAND AND MORROW COUNTIES

944 SURFACE ACRES   14 MILES OF SHORE LINE

Fishing Spots
marked by Darrell Allison

VICINITY MAP

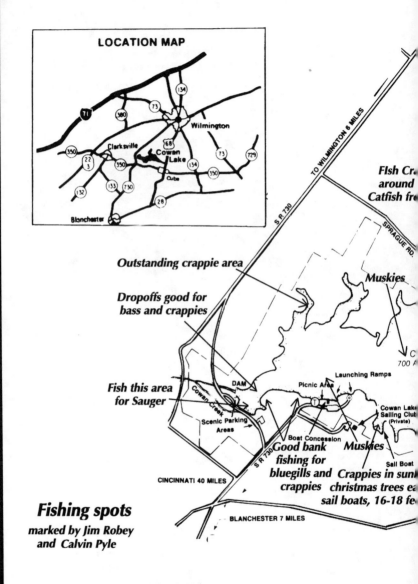

LOCATION MAP

Outstanding crappie area

Dropoffs good for bass and crappies

Fish this area for Sauger

Fish Cr around Catfish fr

Muskies

DAM

Launching Ramps

Picnic Area

Cowan Lake Sailing Club (Private)

Scenic Parking Areas

Boat Concession

Good bank fishing for bluegills and crappies

Muskies

Sail Boat

Crappies in sunk christmas trees ea sail boats, 16-18 fe

Cowan Creek

CINCINNATI 40 MILES

BLANCHESTER 7 MILES

Fishing spots
marked by Jim Robey and Calvin Pyle

TO WILMINGTON 6 MILES

SPRAGUE RD.

S.R. 730

S R 730

C
700 A

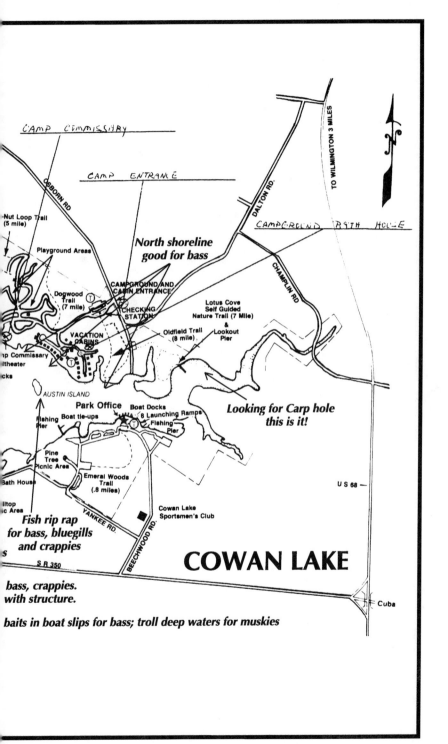

CAMP COMMISSARY

CAMP ENTRANCE

TO WILMINGTON 3 MILES

OSBORN RD.

DALTON RD.

CAMPGROUND BATH HOUSE

-Nut Loop Trail
(5 mile)

Playground Areas

CHAMPLIN RD.

**North shoreline
good for bass**

Dogwood
Trail
(7 mile)

CAMPGROUND AND
CABIN ENTRANCE

CHECKING
STATION

Lotus Cove
Self Guided
Nature Trail (7 Mile)
&
Lookout
Pier

VACATION
CABINS

Oldfield Trail
(8 mile)

p Commissary
itheater

cks

AUSTIN ISLAND

**Looking for Carp hole
this is it!**

Park Office

Boat Docks

8 Launching Ramps

Boat tie-ups

Fishing
Pier

Fishing
Pier

Pine
Tree
Picnic Area

ath House

Emeral Woods
Trail
(.8 miles)

US 68 —

ltop
c Area

**Fish rip rap
for bass, bluegills
and crappies**

Cowan Lake
Sportsmen's Club

s

YANKEE RD.

BEECHWOOD RD.

S R 350

COWAN LAKE

**bass, crappies.
with structure.**

baits in boat slips for bass; troll deep waters for muskies

Cuba

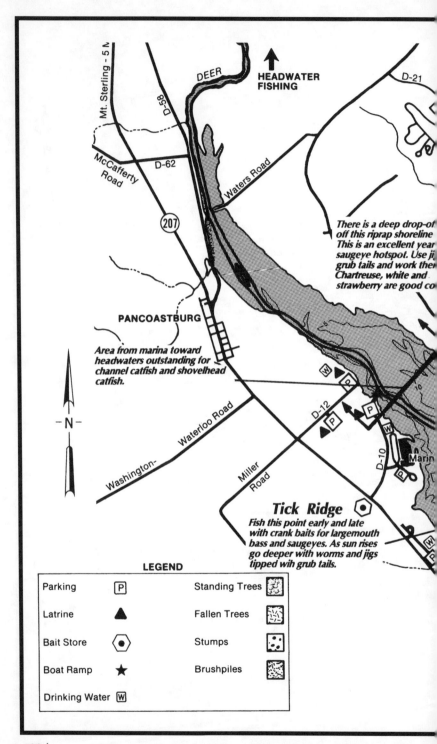

Mt. Sterling - 5 M

DEER

**HEADWATER
FISHING**

D-21

D-58

McCafferty Road

D-62

Waters Road

207

There is a deep drop-of
off this riprap shoreline
This is an excellent year
saugeye hotspot. Use ji
grub tails and work ther
Chartreuse, white and
strawberry are good co

PANCOASTBURG

Area from marina toward
headwaters outstanding for
channel catfish and shovelhead
catfish.

Waterloo Road

D-12

P

Washington-

Miller Road

D-10

Marin

Tick Ridge ⬡
Fish this point early and late
with crank baits for largemouth
bass and saugeyes. As sun rises
go deeper with worms and jigs
tipped wih grub tails.

-N-

LEGEND

Parking	P	Standing Trees	
Latrine	▲	Fallen Trees	
Bait Store	⬡	Stumps	
Boat Ramp	★	Brushpiles	
Drinking Water	W		

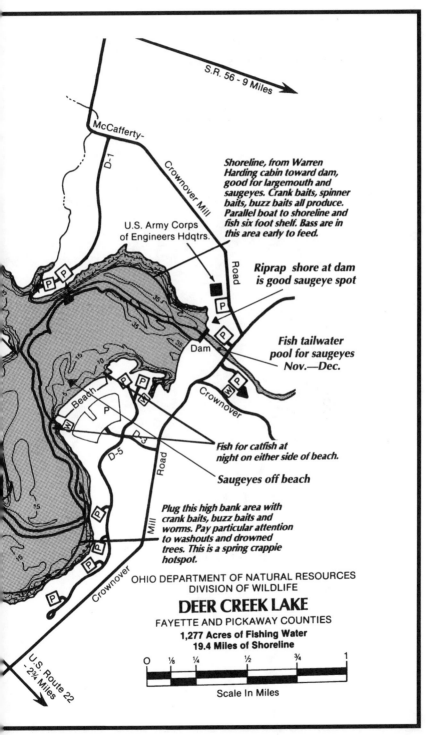

S.R. 56 - 9 Miles

McCafferty-

D-1

Crownover Mill

U.S. Army Corps of Engineers Hdqtrs.

Road

Shoreline, from Warren Harding cabin toward dam, good for largemouth and saugeyes. Crank baits, spinner baits, buzz baits all produce. Parallel boat to shoreline and fish six foot shelf. Bass are in this area early to feed.

Riprap shore at dam is good saugeye spot

Dam

Fish tailwater pool for saugeyes Nov.—Dec.

Crownover

Beach

D-3

D-5

Road

Fish for catfish at night on either side of beach.

Saugeyes off beach

Plug this high bank area with crank baits, buzz baits and worms. Pay particular attention to washouts and drowned trees. This is a spring crappie hotspot.

Mill Road

Crownover

OHIO DEPARTMENT OF NATURAL RESOURCES
DIVISION OF WILDLIFE

DEER CREEK LAKE

FAYETTE AND PICKAWAY COUNTIES

1,277 Acres of Fishing Water
19.4 Miles of Shoreline

0   1/8   1/4   1/2   3/4   1

Scale In Miles

U.S. Route 22 - 2¾ Miles

Fish outlets of channels for perch and look for concentration of boats indicating school of perch has been found.

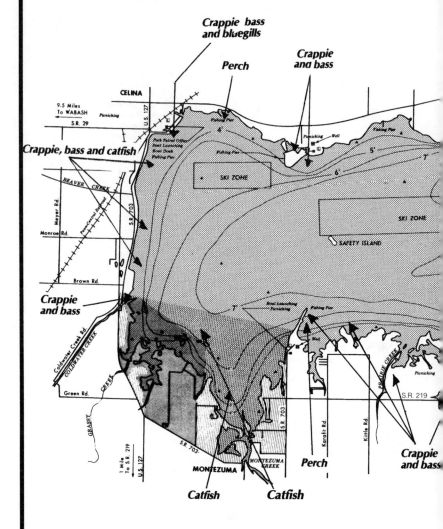

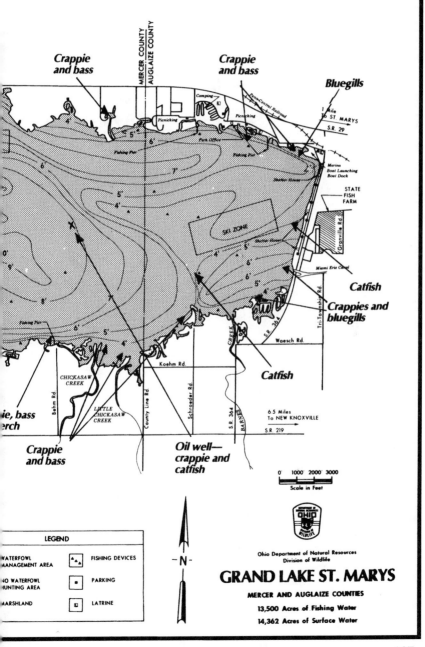

Crappie and bass

Crappie and bass

Bluegills

MERCER COUNTY / AUGLAIZE COUNTY

1 Mile
To ST. MARYS
S.R. 29

Camping

Picnicking

Penn-Central Railroad

Picnicking

Park Office

Fishing Pier

Fishing Pier

Marina
Boat Launching
Boat Dock

Shelter House

STATE
FISH
FARM

SKI ZONE

Granville Rd.

Shelter House

Miami Erie Canal

Catfish

Crappies and bluegills

Fishing Pier

Tri-Township Rd.

S.R. 364

Waesch Rd.

CHICKASAW
CREEK

Koehm Rd.

Catfish

Behm Rd.

LITTLE
CHICKASAW
CREEK

County Line Rd.

Schroeder Rd.

S.R. 364

CREEK

BARNE

6.5 Miles
To NEW KNOXVILLE

S.R. 219

**pie, bass
erch**

Crappie and bass

Oil well— crappie and catfish

0'   1000' 2000' 3000'
Scale in Feet

OHIO
WILDLIFE

Ohio Department of Natural Resources
Division of Wildlife

GRAND LAKE ST. MARYS

MERCER AND AUGLAIZE COUNTIES

13,500 Acres of Fishing Water

14,362 Acres of Surface Water

-N-

LEGEND

WATERFOWL MANAGEMENT AREA	▲▲	FISHING DEVICES
NO WATERFOWL HUNTING AREA	▪	PARKING
MARSHLAND	▣	LATRINE

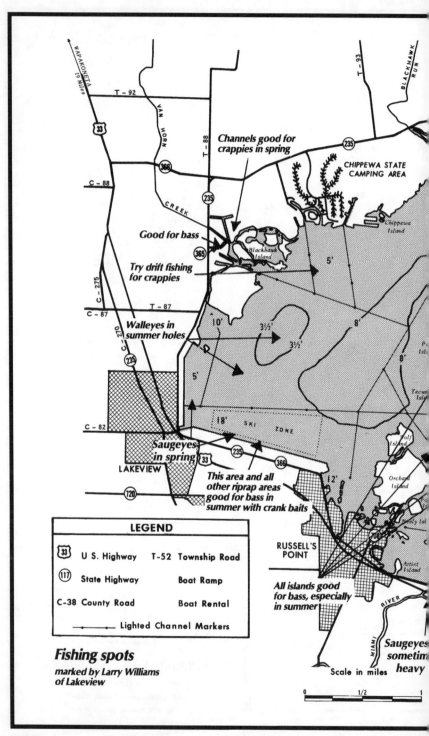

Fishing spots

*marked by Larry Williams
of Lakeview*

LEGEND

33	U S. Highway	T-52	Township Road
117	State Highway		Boat Ramp
C-38	County Road		Boat Rental
		Lighted Channel Markers	

Channels good for crappies in spring

CHIPPEWA STATE CAMPING AREA

Good for bass

Try drift fishing for crappies

Walleyes in summer holes

Saugeyes in spring

LAKEVIEW

This area and all other riprap areas good for bass in summer with crank baits

RUSSELL'S POINT

All islands good for bass, especially in summer

Saugeyes sometim heavy

Scale in miles

108

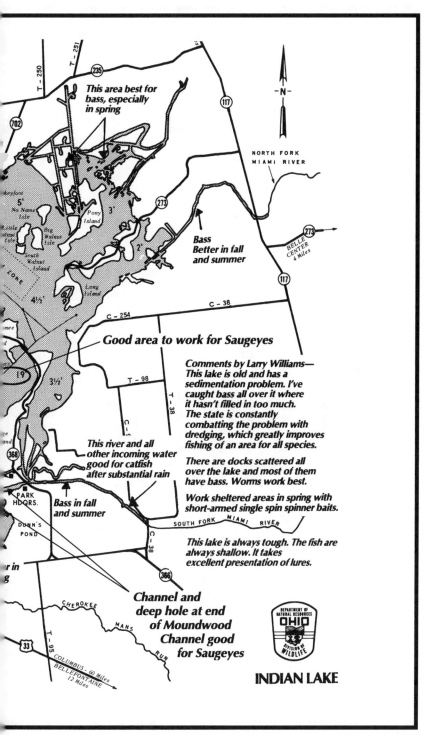

This area best for bass, especially in spring

NORTH FORK MIAMI RIVER

BELLE CENTER 4 Miles

Bass Better in fall and summer

Good area to work for Saugeyes

Comments by Larry Williams—
This lake is old and has a sedimentation problem. I've caught bass all over it where it hasn't filled in too much. The state is constantly combatting the problem with dredging, which greatly improves fishing of an area for all species.

There are docks scattered all over the lake and most of them have bass. Worms work best.

Work sheltered areas in spring with short-armed single spin spinner baits.

This lake is always tough. The fish are always shallow. It takes excellent presentation of lures.

This river and all other incoming water good for catfish after substantial rain

PARK HDQRS.

DUNN'S POND

Bass in fall and summer

SOUTH FORK MIAMI RIVER

CHEROKEE

MANS RUN

COLUMBUS - 60 Miles
BELLEFONTAINE 12 Miles

Channel and deep hole at end of Moundwood Channel good for Saugeyes

DEPARTMENT OF NATURAL RESOURCES
OHIO
DIVISION OF WILDLIFE

INDIAN LAKE

109

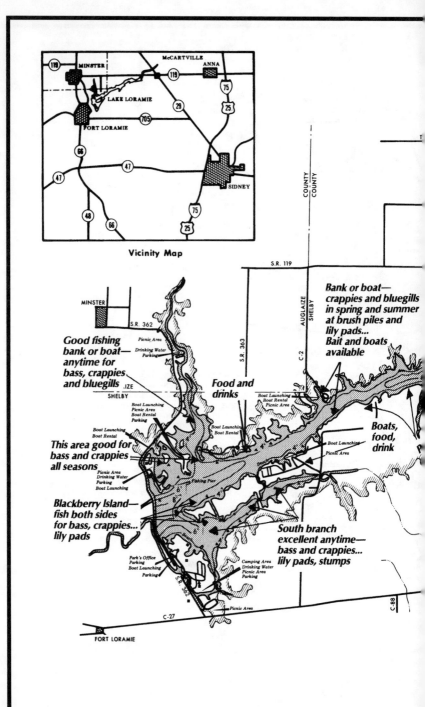

Vicinity Map

MINSTER

S.R. 362

Good fishing bank or boat— anytime for bass, crappies and bluegills

Food and drinks

Bank or boat— crappies and bluegills in spring and summer at brush piles and lily pads... Bait and boats available

This area good for bass and crappies all seasons

Blackberry Island— fish both sides for bass, crappies... lily pads

Boats, food, drink

South branch excellent anytime— bass and crappies... lily pads, stumps

FORT LORAMIE

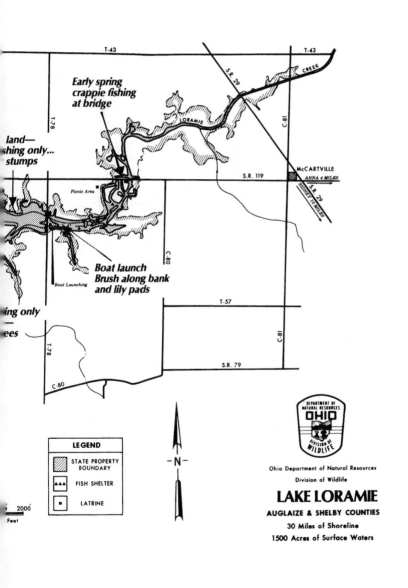

Early spring
crappie fishing
at bridge

land—
shing only...
stumps

Picnic Area

Boat Launching

**Boat launch
Brush along bank
and lily pads**

ing only
—
ees

T-43

T-43

S.R. 29

CREEK

LORAMIE

C-81

McCARTVILLE
ANNA 4 MILES
S.R. 119
SIDNEY 10 MILES
S.R. 29

T-78

T-78

C-80

C-80

C-81

T-57

S.R. 79

2000
Feet

LEGEND

▨	STATE PROPERTY BOUNDARY
▲▲▲	FISH SHELTER
▪	LATRINE

-N-

DEPARTMENT OF
NATURAL RESOURCES
OHIO
DIVISION OF
WILDLIFE

Ohio Department of Natural Resources

Division of Wildlife

LAKE LORAMIE

AUGLAIZE & SHELBY COUNTIES

30 Miles of Shoreline

1500 Acres of Surface Waters

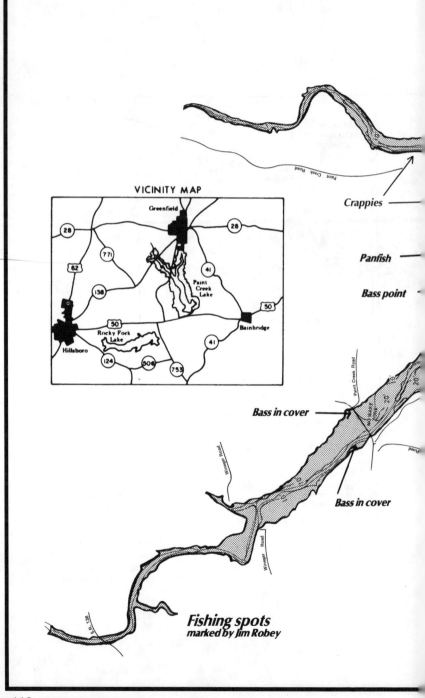

VICINITY MAP

Greenfield

Paint Creek Lake

Hillsboro

Rocky Fork Lake

Bainbridge

Crappies

Panfish

Bass point

Bass in cover

Bass in cover

Fishing spots
marked by Jim Robey

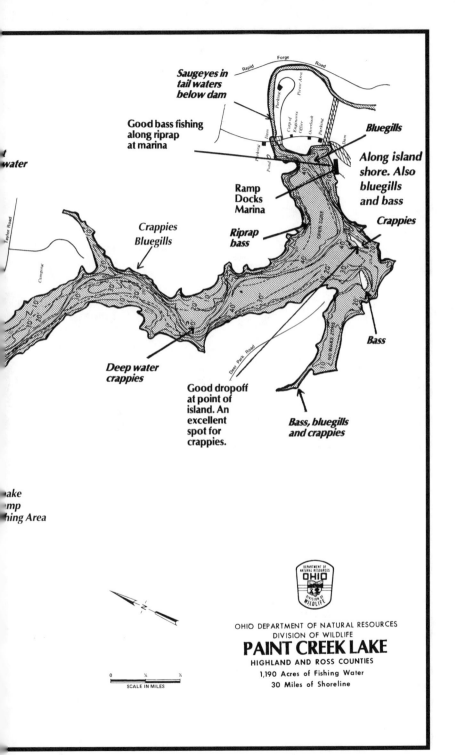

Saugeyes in tail waters below dam

Good bass fishing along riprap at marina

Bluegills

Along island shore. Also bluegills and bass

Crappies

Ramp Docks Marina

Riprap bass

water

Crappies Bluegills

Bass

Deep water crappies

Good dropoff at point of island. An excellent spot for crappies.

Bass, bluegills and crappies

ake mp hing Area

SCALE IN MILES
0   ¼   ½

OHIO DEPARTMENT OF NATURAL RESOURCES
DIVISION OF WILDLIFE
PAINT CREEK LAKE
HIGHLAND AND ROSS COUNTIES
1,190 Acres of Fishing Water
30 Miles of Shoreline

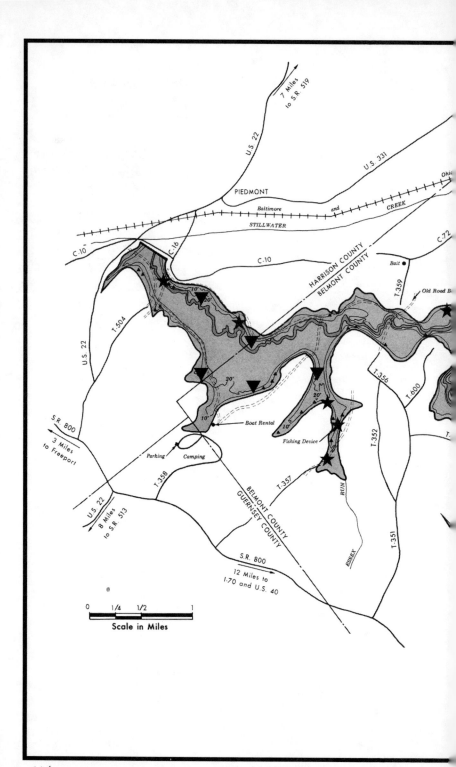

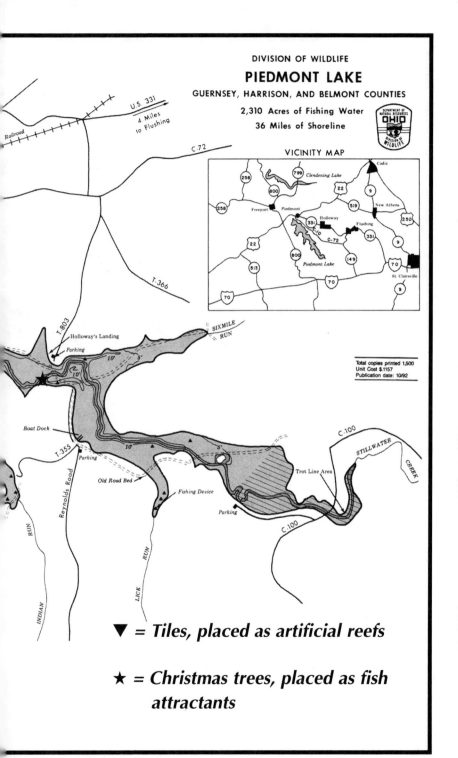

PIEDMONT LAKE

DIVISION OF WILDLIFE

GUERNSEY, HARRISON, AND BELMONT COUNTIES

2,310 Acres of Fishing Water

36 Miles of Shoreline

VICINITY MAP

Total copies printed 1,500
Unit Cost $.1157
Publication date: 10/92

▼ = Tiles, placed as artificial reefs

★ = Christmas trees, placed as fish attractants

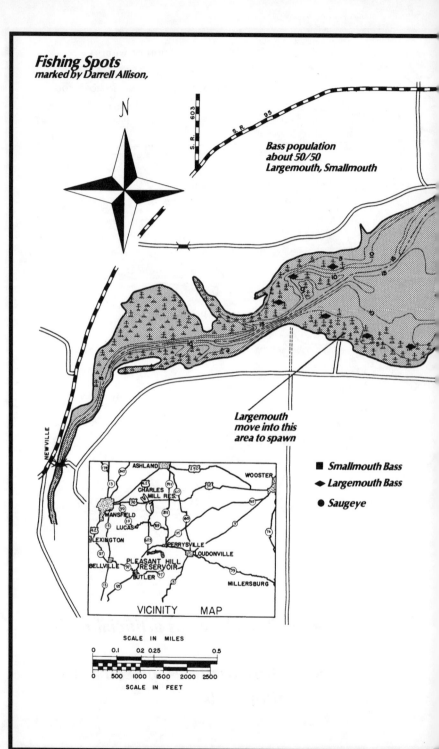

Fishing Spots
marked by Darrell Allison,

N

S.R. 603

S.R. 95

Bass population
about 50/50
Largemouth, Smallmouth

Largemouth
move into this
area to spawn

NEWVILLE

■ Smallmouth Bass
◆ Largemouth Bass
● Saugeye

ASHLAND
WOOSTER
CHARLES MILL RES.
MANSFIELD
LUCAS
LEXINGTON
PERRYSVILLE
LOUDONVILLE
BELLVILLE
PLEASANT HILL RESERVOIR
BUTLER
MILLERSBURG

VICINITY   MAP

SCALE   IN   MILES

0   0.1   0.2 0.25   0.5

0   500   1000   1500   2000   2500

SCALE   IN   FEET

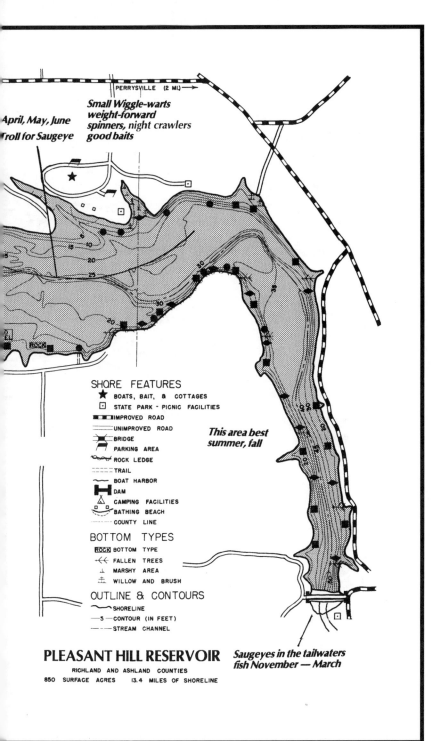

Perrysville (2 Mi) →

Small Wiggle-warts weight-forward spinners, *night crawlers good baits*

April, May, June Troll for Saugeye

This area best summer, fall

SHORE FEATURES

★ BOATS, BAIT, & COTTAGES
⊡ STATE PARK - PICNIC FACILITIES
▬▬ IMPROVED ROAD
── UNIMPROVED ROAD
⌗ BRIDGE
☐ PARKING AREA
∿∿ ROCK LEDGE
∷∷∷ TRAIL
▬ BOAT HARBOR
H DAM
△ CAMPING FACILITIES
⌣ BATHING BEACH
─── COUNTY LINE

BOTTOM TYPES

ROCK BOTTOM TYPE
←← FALLEN TREES
⊥ MARSHY AREA
⊤ WILLOW AND BRUSH

OUTLINE & CONTOURS

∿ SHORELINE
─5─ CONTOUR (IN FEET)
──── STREAM CHANNEL

PLEASANT HILL RESERVOIR

RICHLAND AND ASHLAND COUNTIES
850 SURFACE ACRES   13.4 MILES OF SHORELINE

Saugeyes in the tailwaters fish November — March

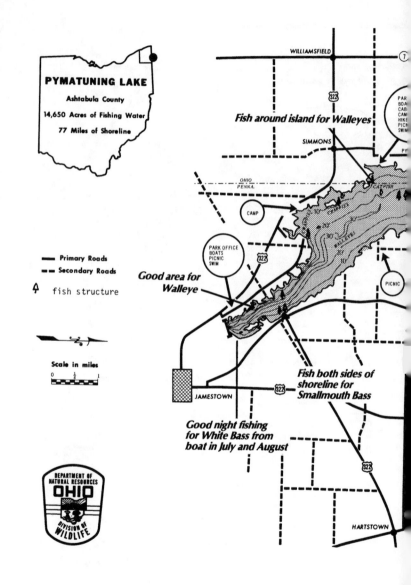

PYMATUNING LAKE

Ashtabula County

14,650 Acres of Fishing Water

77 Miles of Shoreline

Fish around island for Walleyes

WILLIAMSFIELD

SIMMONS

OHIO
PENNA.

CAMP

PARK OFFICE
BOATS
PICNIC
SWIM

—— Primary Roads

-- Secondary Roads

Ϙ   fish structure

Scale in miles

0   ½   1

Good area for Walleye

PICNIC

Fish both sides of shoreline for Smallmouth Bass

JAMESTOWN

Good night fishing for White Bass from boat in July and August

HARTSTOWN

DEPARTMENT OF
NATURAL RESOURCES
OHIO
DIVISION OF
WILDLIFE

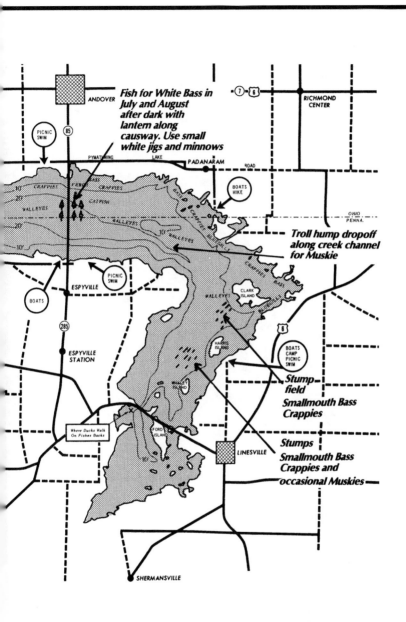

Fish for White Bass in July and August after dark with lantern along causeway. Use small white jigs and minnows

ANDOVER

RICHMOND CENTER

PICNIC SWIM

PYMATUNING LAKE PADANARAM ROAD

BOATS HIKE

CRAPPIES CRAPPIES
CATFISH
WALLEYES
WALLEYES

OHIO
PENNA.

Troll hump dropoff along creek channel for Muskie

PICNIC SWIM

BOATS

ESPYVILLE

WALLEYES

CLARK ISLAND

ESPYVILLE STATION

HARRIS ISLAND

BOATS CAMP PICNIC SWIM

Stump field

Smallmouth Bass
Crappies

Where Ducks Walk On Fishes Backs

WHALEY ISLAND

FORD ISLAND

LINESVILLE

Stumps

Smallmouth Bass
Crappies and
occasional Muskies

SHERMANSVILLE

PYMATUNING LAKE

119

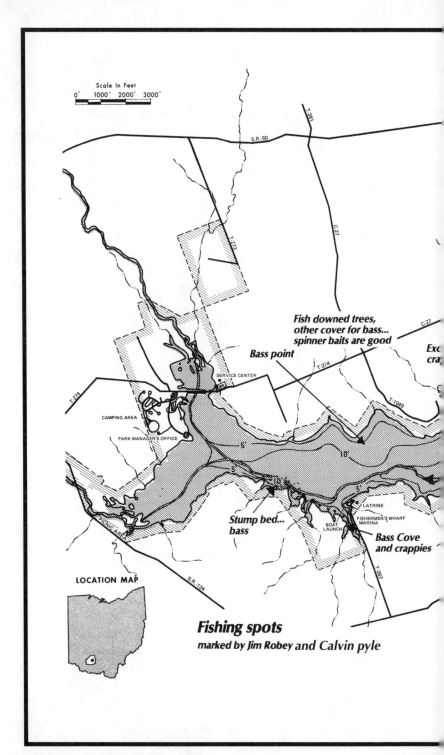

Scale In Feet
0' 1000' 2000' 3000'

Fish downed trees,
other cover for bass...
spinner baits are good

Bass point

Exc
cra

SERVICE CENTER

T-274

T-1049

CAMPING AREA

PARK MANAGER'S OFFICE

5'

10'

5'

10'

5'

PICNIC AREA

10'

LATRINE

FISHERMEN'S WHARF
MARINA

BOAT
LAUNCH

Stump bed...
bass

Bass Cove
and crappies

LOCATION MAP

S.R.-124

S.R.-50

T-281

C-27

C-27

T-213

T-274

T-261

Fishing spots
marked by Jim Robey and Calvin pyle

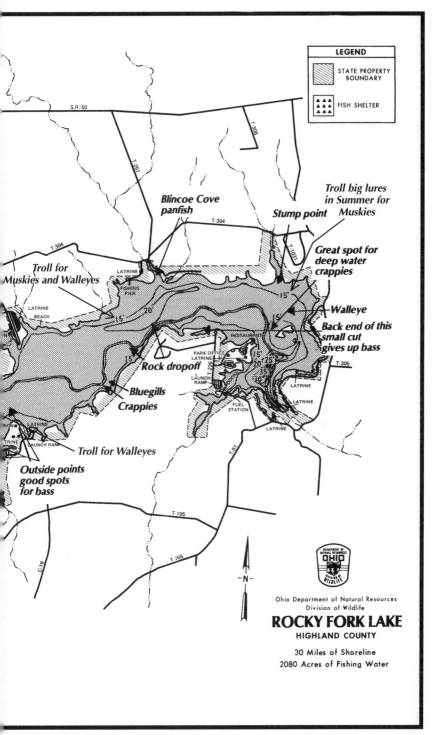

LEGEND

State Property Boundary

Fish Shelter

S.R.-50

T-308

T-251

Troll big lures
in Summer for
Muskies

Blincoe Cove
panfish

Stump point

T-304

T-1031

Great spot for
deep water
crappies

T-304

Troll for
Muskies and Walleyes

LATRINE

FISHING
PIER

15'

20'

15'

15'

Walleye

Back end of this
small cut
gives up bass

LATRINE

BEACH

RESTAURANT

PARK OFFICE
LATRINE

T-305

15'

Rock dropoff

25'

20'

25'

LAUNCH
RAMP

35'

30'

LATRINE

Bluegills

Crappies

FUEL
STATION

LATRINE

LATRINE

LATRINE

LATRINE

LAUNCH RAMP

Troll for Walleyes

T-51

Outside points
good spots
for bass

T-195

C-19

T-205

—N—

Ohio Department of Natural Resources
Division of Wildlife

ROCKY FORK LAKE

HIGHLAND COUNTY

30 Miles of Shoreline
2080 Acres of Fishing Water

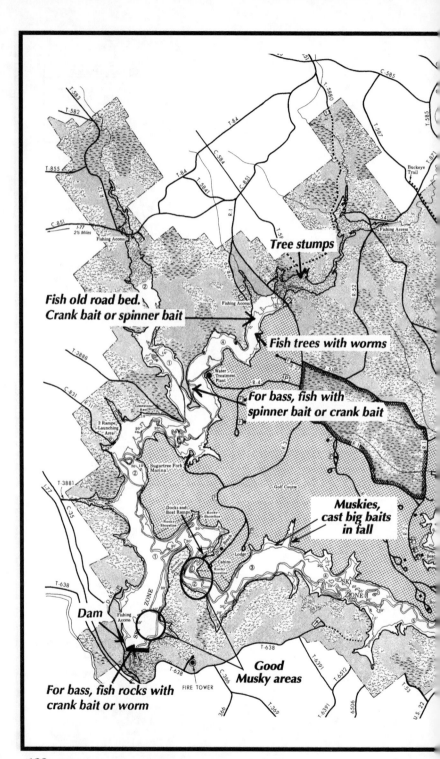

Tree stumps

Fish old road bed. Crank bait or spinner bait

Fish trees with worms

For bass, fish with spinner bait or crank bait

Muskies, cast big baits in fall

Dam

Good Musky areas

For bass, fish rocks with crank bait or worm

FIRE TOWER

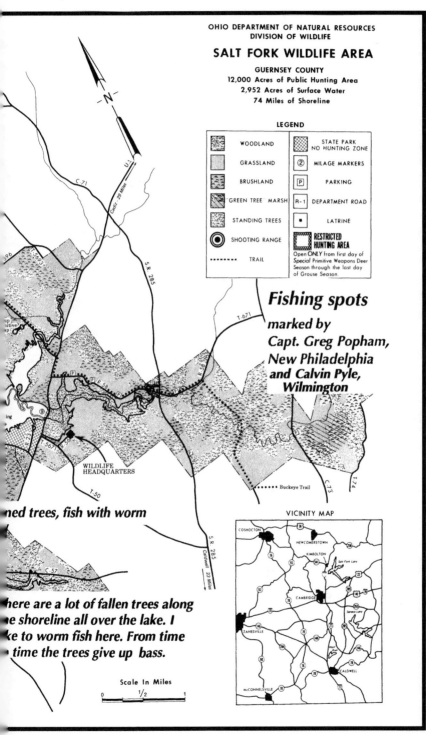

OHIO DEPARTMENT OF NATURAL RESOURCES
DIVISION OF WILDLIFE

SALT FORK WILDLIFE AREA

GUERNSEY COUNTY
12,000 Acres of Public Hunting Area
2,952 Acres of Surface Water
74 Miles of Shoreline

LEGEND

	WOODLAND		STATE PARK NO HUNTING ZONE
	GRASSLAND	②	MILAGE MARKERS
	BRUSHLAND	P	PARKING
	GREEN TREE MARSH	R-1	DEPARTMENT ROAD
	STANDING TREES	▪	LATRINE
	SHOOTING RANGE		**RESTRICTED HUNTING AREA**
....	TRAIL		Open ONLY from first day of *Special* Primitive Weapons Deer Season through the last day of Grouse Season.

Fishing spots

*marked by
Capt. Greg Popham,
New Philadelphia
and Calvin Pyle,
Wilmington*

●●●●● Buckeye Trail

WILDLIFE
HEADQUARTERS

ned trees, fish with worm

*here are a lot of fallen trees along
he shoreline all over the lake. I
ke to worm fish here. From time
 time the trees give up bass.*

VICINITY MAP

Scale In Miles
0   ½   1

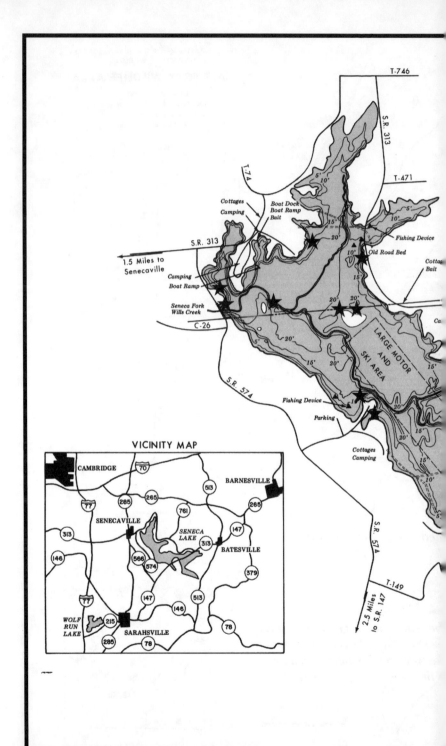

T-746

S.R. 313

T-471

Cottages
Camping

Boat Dock
Boat Ramp
Bait

5'
10'

5'
10'

Fishing Device

S.R. 313

Old Road Bed

10'

Cottas
Bait

1.5 Miles to
Senecaville

15'

Camping
Boat Ramp

20'

20'

20'

Ca

Seneca Fork
Wills Creek

LARGE MOTOR
AND
SKI AREA

C-26

5'

20'

15'

20'

15'

S.R. 57A

15'

20'

Fishing Device

Parking

20'

15'

Cottages
Camping

20'

15'

15'

S.R. 57A

10'

VICINITY MAP

5'

CAMBRIDGE — 70

BARNESVILLE

77

285

265

513

265

761

SENECAVILLE

SENECA
LAKE

147

313

381

BATESVILLE

566

574

379

146

T-149

2.5 Miles
to S.R. 147

77

147

513

146

WOLF
RUN
LAKE

215

78

SARAHSVILLE

285

78

124

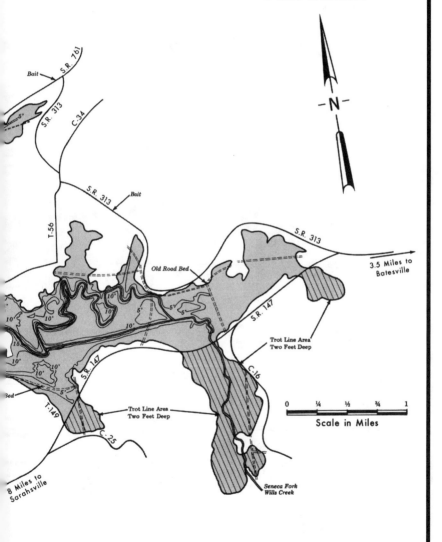

★ = *Christmas trees used as fish attractants (60 trees per site.)*

OHIO DEPARTMENT OF NATURAL RESOURCES
DIVISION OF WILDLIFE

SENECA LAKE

GUERNSEY AND NOBLE COUNTIES

3,550 Acres of Fishing Water
47 Miles of Shoreline

-N-

S.R. 761

Bait

S.R. 313

C.34

S.R. 313

Bait

T-56

S.R. 313

3.5 Miles to Batesville

Old Road Bed

10'

10'
10'

5'

5'

S.R. 147

Trot Line Area
Two Feet Deep

15'

10'
10'

S.R. 147

C.16

Bed

T-149

Trot Line Area
Two Feet Deep

0   ¼   ½   ¾   1

Scale in Miles

C.25

8 Miles to
Sarahsville

Seneca Fork
Wills Creek

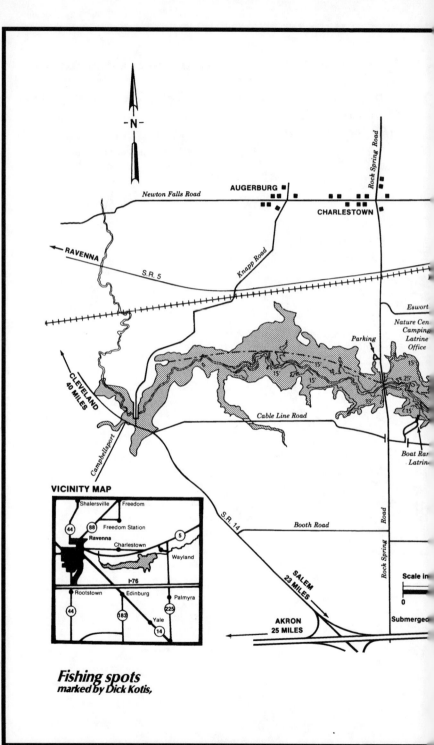

Fishing spots
marked by Dick Kotis,

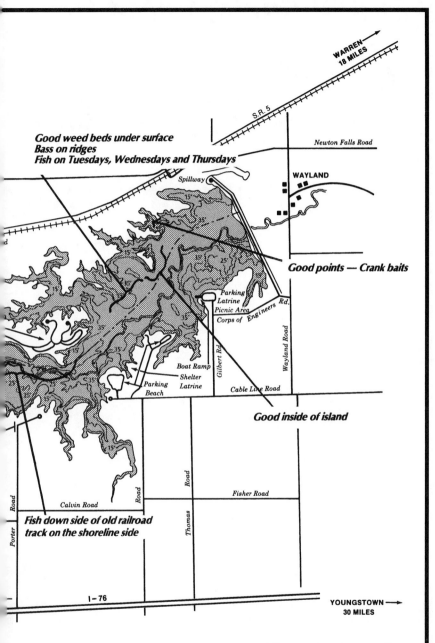

Good weed beds under surface
Bass on ridges
Fish on Tuesdays, Wednesdays and Thursdays

WARREN
18 MILES

S.R. 5

Newton Falls Road

WAYLAND

Spillway

Good points — Crank baits

Parking
Latrine
Picnic Area
Corps of Engineers Rd.

Wayland Road

Boat Ramp
Shelter
Latrine
Parking
Beach

Gilbert Rd.

Cable Line Road

Good inside of island

Calvin Road

Road

Thomas Road

Fisher Road

Porter Road

Fish down side of old railroad
track on the shoreline side

I - 76

YOUNGSTOWN →
30 MILES

WEST BRANCH RESERVOIR

PORTAGE COUNTY

2350 Acres of Surface Area
40 Miles of Shoreline

127

Ohio's Record Fish

Hook-and-Line All-Time Fishing Records,
as compiled by the Outdoor Writers of Ohio.
Records are based on heaviest weight.
Fish must be photographed, witnessed, weighed on certified scale and kept frozen until record is verified. For further information contact: Jeff Frischkorn, Outdoor Writers of Ohio, 7612 Dahlia Drive, Mentor-on-the-Lake, OH 44060. Phone 216-257-2483.

LARGEMOUTH BASS
Pugnacious attitude makes it the most popular
game fish in North America

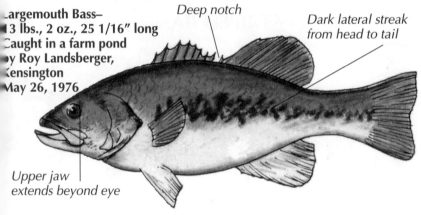

Largemouth Bass–
13 lbs., 2 oz., 25 1/16" long
Caught in a farm pond
by Roy Landsberger,
Kensington
May 26, 1976

Deep notch

Dark lateral streak from head to tail

Upper jaw extends beyond eye

SMALLMOUTH BASS
A great fighter likely
to put on an aerial display

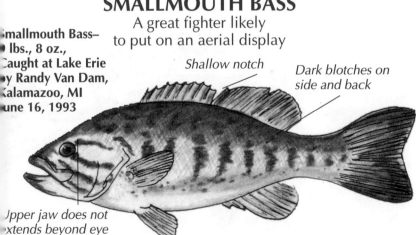

Smallmouth Bass–
9 lbs., 8 oz.,
Caught at Lake Erie
by Randy Van Dam,
Kalamazoo, MI
June 16, 1993

Shallow notch

Dark blotches on side and back

Upper jaw does not extends beyond eye

129

SPOTTED BASS

This spunky fighter is easily confused with
the more common largemouth bass

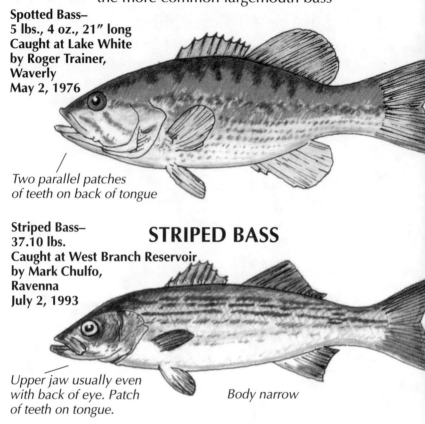

**Spotted Bass–
5 lbs., 4 oz., 21″ long
Caught at Lake White
by Roger Trainer,
Waverly
May 2, 1976**

*Two parallel patches
of teeth on back of tongue*

STRIPED BASS

**Striped Bass–
37.10 lbs.
Caught at West Branch Reservoir
by Mark Chulfo,
Ravenna
July 2, 1993**

*Upper jaw usually even
with back of eye. Patch
of teeth on tongue.*

Body narrow

HYBRID STRIPED BASS

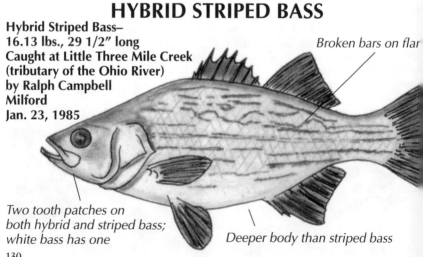

**Hybrid Striped Bass–
16.13 lbs., 29 1/2″ long
Caught at Little Three Mile Creek
(tributary of the Ohio River)
by Ralph Campbell
Milford
Jan. 23, 1985**

Broken bars on flar

*Two tooth patches on
both hybrid and striped bass;
white bass has one*

Deeper body than striped bass

WHITE BASS
Excellent light-tackle game fish that will take bait or lure

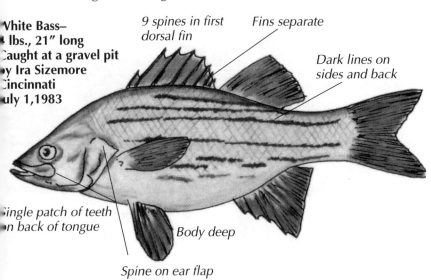

White Bass–
4 lbs., 21" long
Caught at a gravel pit
by Ira Sizemore
Cincinnati
July 1,1983

9 spines in first dorsal fin

Fins separate

Dark lines on sides and back

Single patch of teeth on back of tongue

Body deep

Spine on ear flap

WHITE PERCH

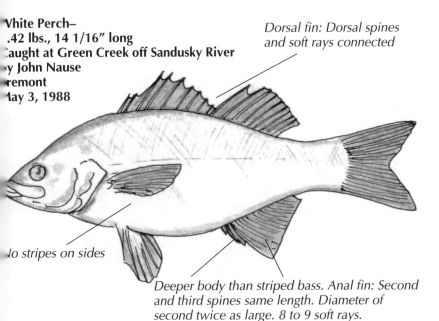

White Perch–
.42 lbs., 14 1/16" long
Caught at Green Creek off Sandusky River
by John Nause
Fremont
May 3, 1988

Dorsal fin: Dorsal spines and soft rays connected

No stripes on sides

Deeper body than striped bass. Anal fin: Second and third spines same length. Diameter of second twice as large. 8 to 9 soft rays.

ROCK BASS

A robust sunfish that looks like a cross
between a bluegill and a bass

Rock Bass–
1 lb., 15 1/2 oz., 14 3/4″ long
Caught at Deer Creek
near London
by George A. Keller
Dayton
Sept. 3, 1962

Shallow notch

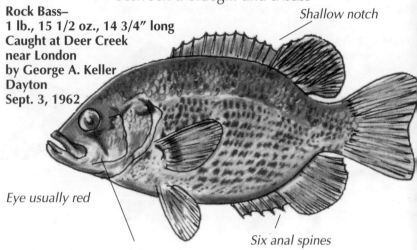

Eye usually red

Six anal spines

*Upper jaw extends beyond
front edge of eye*

BLUEGILL

Ounce for ounce,
one of the scrappiest sport fish

Bluegill–
3 lbs., 4 1/2 oz., 12 3/4″ long
Caught at Salt Fork Lake
by Willis D. Nicholes
Quaker City
April 28, 1990

*Black blotch on back
of dorsal fin*

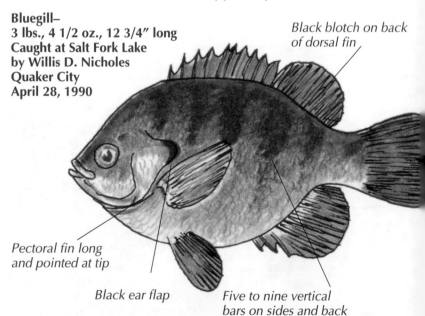

*Pectoral fin long
and pointed at tip*

Black ear flap

*Five to nine vertical
bars on sides and back*

BOWFIN
This fish that has journeyed through the ages
is considered a living fossil

Bowfin–
11 lbs., 7 oz., 33 1/4″ long
Caught at Nettle Lake
by Chris Boling
Montpelier
May 9, 1987

Dorsal fin more than
half of body length

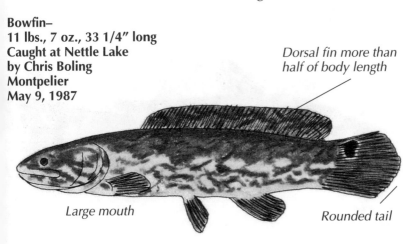

Large mouth

Rounded tail

CARP
Asian fish made it to America by way of
Europe in the late 1880's

Carp–
50 lbs., 40″ long
Caught at Paint Creek
by Judson Holton
Chillicothe
May 24, 1967

Hard sawtoothed spine

Long dorsal fin

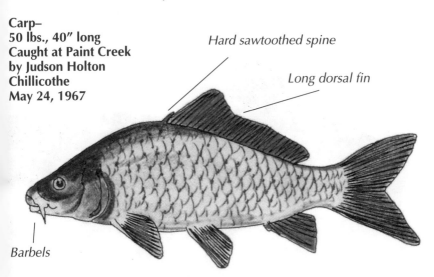

Barbels

Hard sawtoothed spine

BLACK BULLHEAD
Spawning males are jet black

Bullhead– (includes all bullhead catfish)
4 lbs., 4 oz., 18 1/2″ long
Caught at farm pond
by Hugh Lawrence Jr.
Keene
May 20, 1986

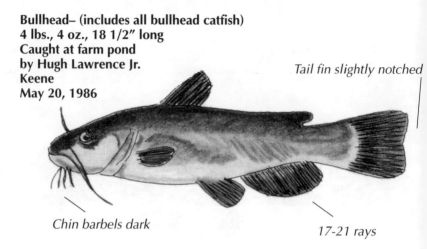

Tail fin slightly notched

Chin barbels dark

17-21 rays

BROWN BULLHEAD
Found in larger and deeper waters than other bullheads

Be extra careful when releasing a catfish. It has a sharp horn on each side of its body and one on its back.

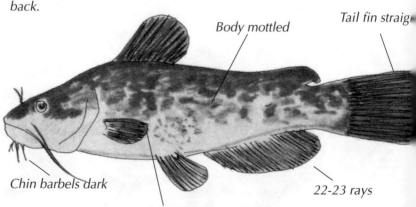

Body mottled

Tail fin straig

Chin barbels dark

22-23 rays

Strong barbs on back of pectoral fins

YELLOW BULLHEAD
This is the true-yellow belly bullhead

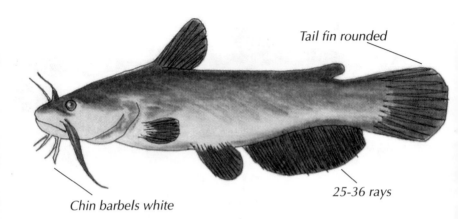

Tail fin rounded

Chin barbels white

25-36 rays

CHANNEL CATFISH
Highly regarded for its
food and fighting ability

**Channel Catfish–
37 lbs., 10.4 oz.
Caught at LaDue Reservoir
by Gus J. Gronowski
Parma
Aug. 15, 1992**

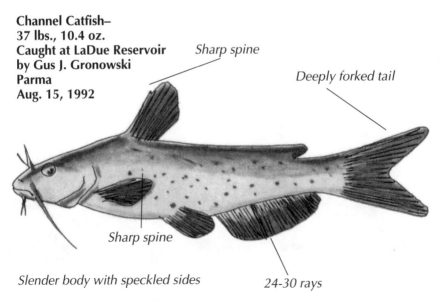

Sharp spine

Deeply forked tail

Sharp spine

Slender body with speckled sides

24-30 rays

FLATHEAD CATFISH
The largest catfish found in Ohio

Flathead Catfish–
76 lbs., 8 oz., 53 5/8" long
Caught at Clendening Lake
by Richard Affolter
New Philadelphia
July 28, 1979

Tail fin Rounded or straight

Chin barbels white   *Lower jaw extends below upper jaw*

14-17 rays

Burbot–
9 3/4 lbs., 32 1/4" long
Caught at Lake Erie
by Thomas Franjesh
Akron
Dec. 26,
1994

BURBOT
Long eel-like body

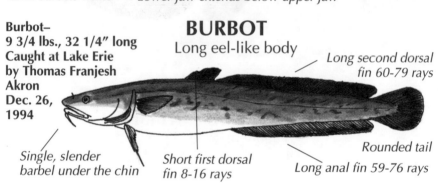

Long second dorsal fin 60-79 rays

Single, slender barbel under the chin   *Short first dorsal fin 8-16 rays*

Rounded tail

Long anal fin 59-76 rays

FRESHWATER DRUM (SHEEPSHEAD)

Freshwater Drum–
22 lbs., 4 oz., 33 1/2" long
Caught in Muskingum River
by Jerry Stack
Macksburg
May 12, 1980

Its humped back and blunt snout
have caused some people
to mistake this fish for a carp

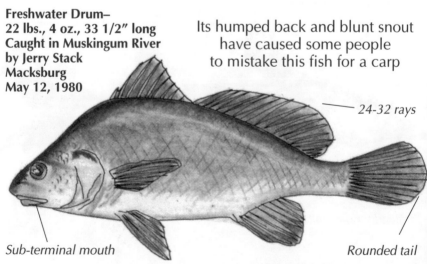

24-32 rays

Sub-terminal mouth

Rounded tail

BLACK CRAPPIE
This crappie has a preference for clear,
weedy lakes or large streams and ponds

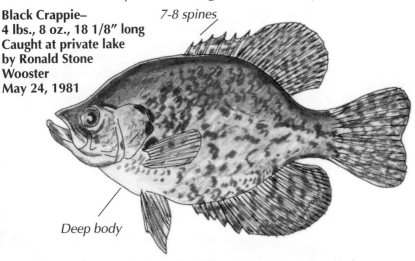

**Black Crappie–
4 lbs., 8 oz., 18 1/8″ long
Caught at private lake
by Ronald Stone
Wooster
May 24, 1981**

7-8 spines

Deep body

WHITE CRAPPIE
This aggressive fighter appeals to anglers of all ages

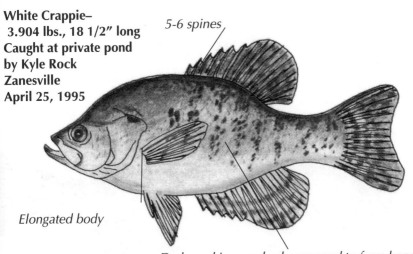

**White Crappie–
3.904 lbs., 18 1/2″ long
Caught at private pond
by Kyle Rock
Zanesville
April 25, 1995**

5-6 spines

Elongated body

Dark markings on body arranged to form bands

GAR, Any Species
The eggs of this primitive fish are poisonous to humans

**Longnose Gar–
25 lbs., 49" long
Caught in the Ohio River
by Flora Irvin**

Diamond-shaped bony plate-like scales

**Cincinnati
Aug. 31,1996**

Narrow snout, sharp teeth

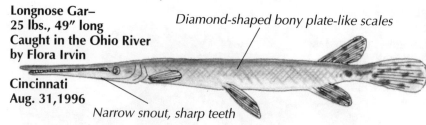

MUSKELLUNGE

**Muskellunge–
(pure strain)
55 lbs., 2 oz., 50 1/4" long
Caught at Piedmont Lake
by Joe D. Lykins
Piedmont
April 12, 1972**

Cheeks and gill cover are usually scaled on top half

**Muskellunge–
(Tiger)
26 lbs., 8 oz., 45" long
Caught at West Branch Reservoir
by James Prettyman
Suffield
Aug. 25, 1984**

Musky has 6-9 pores under lower jaw on each side

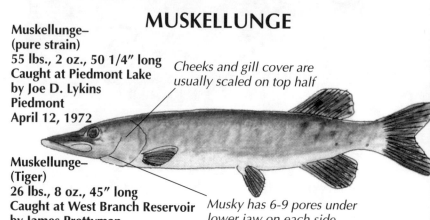

YELLOW PERCH

**Yellow Perch–
2 lbs., 12 oz., 14 1/2" long
Caught at Lake Erie
by Charles Thomas
Lorain
April 17, 1984**

Fins separate

Sides bright yellow

Seven blackish bars crossing sides

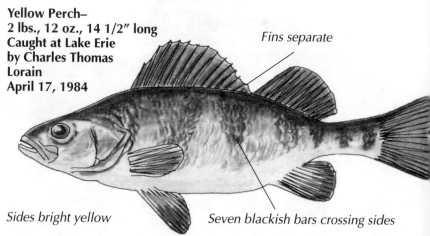

CHAIN PICKEREL
This member of the pike family
has a limited range in Ohio

**Chain Pickerel–
6 lbs., 4 oz., 26 1/4" long
Caught at Long Lake
by Ronald Kotch
Akron
March 25, 1961**

*Cheek and gill covers
are fully scaled*

Deeply forked tail

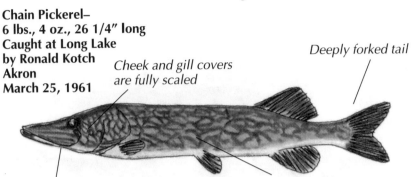

*Pickerel usually has 4 pores
on each side of lower jaw*

Chain-like reticulations on body

NORTHERN PIKE
A long, sleek predatory fish
with a mouth full of teeth

**Northern Pike–
22 lbs., 6 oz., 43" long
Caught at Lyre Lake (Fairborn, Ohio)
by Chris Campbell
Dayton
Oct., 3, 1988**

Upper half of gill covers scaled

Cheek fully scaled

*Pike usually has 5 pores on
each side of lower jaw*

Light colored spots on body

REDEAR SUNFISH
Pugnacious sunfish has big appetite

Redear Sunfish–
3 lbs., 1 oz., 13 1/4″ long
Caught at a pond in Muskingum Co.
by Terry J. Paisley
Zanesville
May 28, 1988

Soft dorsal fin

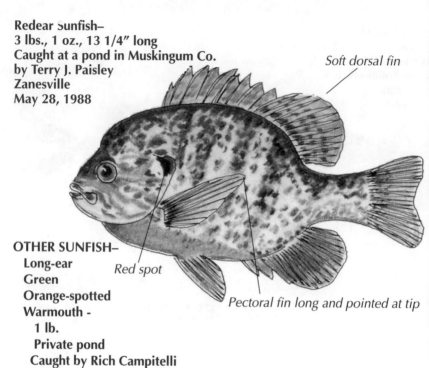

OTHER SUNFISH–
   Long-ear
   Green
   Orange-spotted
   Warmouth -
      1 lb.
   Private pond
   Caught by Rich Campitelli
   Athens
   Sept. 6, 1994

Red spot

Pectoral fin long and pointed at tip

CHINOOK SALMON

Chinook Salmon–
29 lbs., 8 oz., 42 7/8″ long
Caught at Lake Erie
by Walter Shumaker
Ashtabula
Aug. 4, 1989

Spots occur on top of head

Many spots on upper body and fins

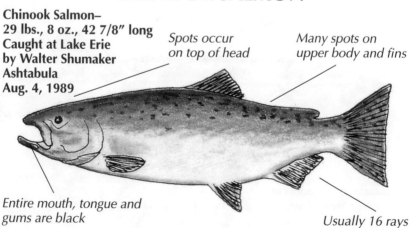

Entire mouth, tongue and gums are black

Usually 16 rays

COHO SALMON
One of the best fighters,
also known as the silver salmon

**Coho Salmon–
13 lbs., 10 oz., 34 3/4" long
Caught in the Huron River
by Barney Freeman, Kansas
Dec. 1, 1982**

*Spots on upper
lobe of tail*

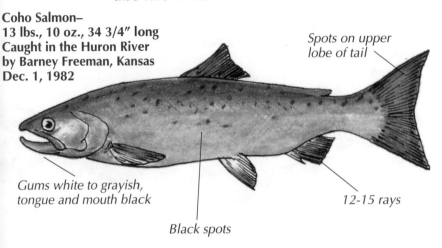

*Gums white to grayish,
tongue and mouth black*

Black spots

12-15 rays

SAUGER
This close relative of the walleye is found
in the Ohio River and its tributaries

**Sauger–
7 lbs., 5 oz., 24 1/2" long
Caught in the Maumee River
by Bryan Wicks
Maumee
March 10, 1981**

Spinous dorsal fin with distinct dark spots

17-20 rays

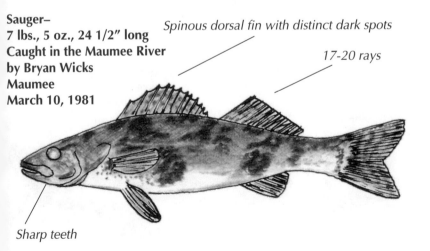

Sharp teeth

SAUGEYE
This walleye-sauger cross is bringing
year-round fishing pleasures to Ohio

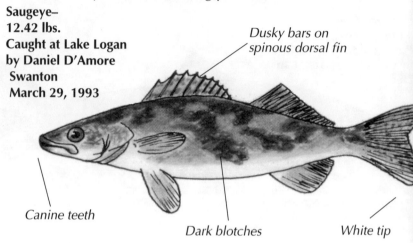

**Saugeye–
12.42 lbs.
Caught at Lake Logan
by Daniel D'Amore
Swanton
March 29, 1993**

*Dusky bars on
spinous dorsal fin*

Canine teeth

Dark blotches

White tip

WALLEYE
For many, Ohio's
number one sport fish

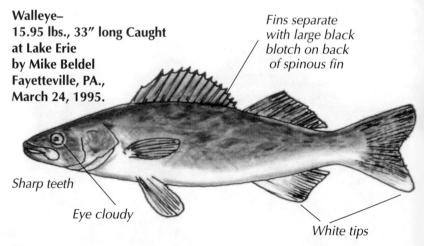

**Walleye–
15.95 lbs., 33″ long Caught
at Lake Erie
by Mike Beldel
Fayetteville, PA.,
March 24, 1995.**

*Fins separate
with large black
blotch on back
of spinous fin*

Sharp teeth

Eye cloudy

White tips

SUCKER

Fishing season begins for many when
suckers are found in stream riffles

ffalo Sucker–
 lbs., 1 oz., 38 " long
ught at Hoover Reservoir
 David Heinselman
hanna
ly 3, 1988

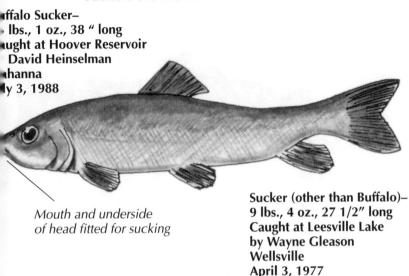

*Mouth and underside
of head fitted for sucking*

**Sucker (other than Buffalo)–
9 lbs., 4 oz., 27 1/2" long
Caught at Leesville Lake
by Wayne Gleason
Wellsville
April 3, 1977**

BROOK TROUT

Colorful markings make this one of
the most beautiful fresh water fish

k Trout–
., 11 oz., 18 1/2 " long
ht in the East Branch of the Chagrin River
 Graboshek
ughby
30, 1955

Square tail

Wormlike markings

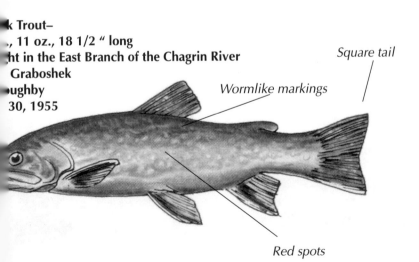

Red spots

BROWN TROUT
This trout was considered a trash fish by many anglers when first introduced

**Brown trout–
14.65 lbs., 25 1/4 in. long
Caught at Lake Erie
by Timothy L. Byme,
Brooklyn, MI
July 15, 1995**

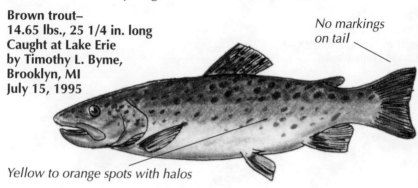

No markings on tail

Yellow to orange spots with halos

**Lake trout–
16 lbs., 11 oz.
Caught at Lake Erie
by Daniel Wilson, Hudson
June 6, 1993**

LAKE TROUT

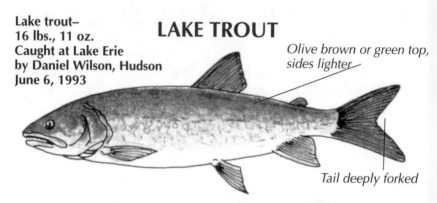

Olive brown or green top, sides lighter

Tail deeply forked

RAINBOW TROUT AND/OR STEELHEAD
This fish is the best known member of the trout family

**Rainbow–
20.97 lbs., 36 1/2 in. long
Caught at Lake Erie
by Mike Shane,
New Middletown,
Oct. 2,1996**

Dark spots

Broad red or pink band along sides

10-12 rays

Campers at Paint Creek Lake have view of water from an inviting campground.

Fishing and camping make a good combo

By Jim Robey

Salt Fork State Park near Cambridge would get a high rating from anyone who wanted to combine a fishing trip with camping, and thousands of people are doing it.

With 212 campsites in one of Ohio's most inviting parks, and each site with an electric outlet, Salt Fork is an appealing place for the tent camper or RV owner.

Add to this the angling opportunity in one of Ohio's top all-around fishing lakes (see Salt Fork in the lake section) and you have an outstanding camp-and-fish destination.

Many Ohio State Parks with camping services are close to prime fishing. The campgrounds at East Harbor and the ones on the Bass Islands are at the doorstep of the greatest walleye fishing in the world, not to mention the finest smallmouth bass fishing you can find.

Campers at Grand Lake St. Marys know they are minutes away from superb crappie fishing. The saugeye explosion at Indian Lake is luring more campers to that park.

In fact, with nearly 60 state parks serving campers, the traveling angler who wants to go someplace for a weekend or longer can find good camping facilities next to, or close to his favorite lake.

Overnight camping fees at state parks range from $8 a night for a non-electric site at a park with limited facilities to $15 a night for a park such as Salt Fork that has everything from modern bathhouses to a swimming beach, not to mention trails, golf course, cabins and lodge.

The Ohio Fishing Guide's directory of state parks with campgrounds has all the information you need. In it you'll find the location of the parks, size of each, amount of water, address, phone number and whether the park offers Rent-A-Camp or Rent-A-RV.

Campground at South Bass Island places anglers close to good fishing.

Camping is easy with RENT-A-Camp or RENT-A-RV

By Jim Robey

The Ohio Division of Parks and Recreation provides a way to experience tent camping at an Ohio State Park in an easy, inexpensive way: It's Rent-A-Camp, and it costs from $20 to $27 per night, depending on the park visited.

Another option is the new Rent-A-RV at East Fork, Caesar Creek, Punderson and Geneva where you can visit a popular park and have the comforts of home for $55 a night, or as little as $45 when remaining for seven consecutive nights. At Alum Creek the fee is $65.

Whether staying in a tent or an RV, having a home-away-from-home ready for immediate occupancy when you

arrive is very convenient. Moreover, it's a way to sample camping as a form of family recreation before purchasing a tent or RV.

When campers arrive at their tent site, a 10' x 12' lodge-type tent is already set on a wooden platform and a 12-foot square dining fly shelters a picnic table. The large tent sleeps four adults or two adults and three children. Other pieces of equipment include two cots, two six-foot foam sleeping pads, a 60-quart cooler, a two-burner propane stove and fuel, a camp light, a fire ring and fire extinguisher, plus a throw mat, broom and dust pan.

Rental Season

1. Rent-A-Camp sites are available from May 1 through September 30. Some Rent-A-Camp parks extend their season through October.

2. Reservations are accepted as early as March 1. They must be made through the mail. Although phone reservations are not accepted, you may want to call the park or parks of your choice to request an application and check on the availability of sites.

3. Reservations are not accepted for longer than one week for Rent-A-Camp, but Rent-A-RV, Rent-A-Tepee or Rent-A-Houseboat at Paint Creek can be extended for 14 days.

4. For Rent-A-Camp only, Golden Buckeye cardholders are given a 50 percent discount on their bill when staying from Sunday through Thursday nights, and 10 percent on Friday and Saturday nights.

5. Rental day begins at 4 p.m. on check-in day. Check-out time is 3 p.m. on the last day of reservation.

6. Rent-A-Camp prices are based on the amenities available in a campground.

7. A Rent-A-Camp and Rent-A-RV deposits are equal to one night's rental. Deposits are non-refundable for all confirmed reservations.

Rent-A-Camp and Other Camping Options

Park	County	# of Sites	Cost	Electricity	Showers	Flush Toilets	Alternative # Available	Hiking Trails (mi.)	Swimming	Boat Rental	Launch Ramp	Power Limits	Park Address	Park Office Telephone Number	Park Office FAX Number
Alum Creek	Delaware	5†	$26	X	X	X	■5,●2	8.5	X	X	X	UNL	3615 S. Old State Road, Delaware, 43015-9673	(614) 548-4631	(614) 548-4509
Barkcamp	Belmont	5	$20	-	X	-	-	4	X	-	X	EMO	65330 Barkcamp Park Road, Belmont, 43718-9733	(614) 484-4064	(614) 484-4177
Beaver Creek	Columbiana	2	$20	-	-	-	-	16	-	-	-	-	12021 Echo Dell Road, East Liverpool, 43920-9713	(330) 385-3091	(330) 385-1088
Blue Rock	Muskingum	3	$20	-	●	-	-	3	X	X	X	EMO	7924 Cutler Lake Road, Blue Rock, 43720-9728	(614) 674-4794	(614) 674-6747
Burr Oak	Athens/Morgan	3	$22	X	X	X	-	28	X	X	X	10hp	10220 Burr Oak Lodge Road, Glouster, 45732-9589	(614) 767-3570	(614) 767-3510
Caesar Creek	Warren/Clinton	4	$26	X	X	X	■3	38	X	●●	X	UNL	8570 East S.R. 73, Waynesville, 45068-9719	(513) 897-3055	(513) 897-2733
Deer Creek	Pickaway	5	$27	X	X	X	-	7	X	X	X	UNL	20635 Waterloo Road, Mt. Sterling, 43143-9501	(614) 869-3124	(614) 869-3608
Delaware	Delaware	3	$27	X	X	X	-	7.5	X	X	X	UNL	5202 U.S. 23 North, Delaware, 43015-9714	(614) 369-2761	(614) 363-7055
Dillon	Muskingum	2	$27	X	X	X	-	7	X	X	X	UNL	P.O. Box 126, Nashport, 43830-0126	(614) 453-4377	(614) 453-3872
East Fork	Clermont	6†	$26	X	X	X	■6	71	X	●●	X	UNL	Box 119, Bethel, 45106-0119	(513) 734-4323	(513) 734-6166
East Harbor	Ottawa	2	$24	-	X	X	-	7	-	-	X	◆	1169 N. Buck Rd., Lakeside-Marblehead, 43440-9610	(419) 734-5857	(419) 734-2011
Findley	Lorain	3	$23	-	X	X	-	10	X	X	X	EMO	25381 S.R. 58, Wellington, 44090-9208	(216) 647-4490	(216) 647-6318
Forked Run	Meigs	4	$20	-	X	-	-	3	X	X	X	10hp /◆	P.O. Box 127, Reedsville, 45772-0127	(614) 378-6206	(614) 378-6306
Geneva	Ashtabula	3	$27	X	X	X	■3	3	X	●●	X	◆	Padanarum Road, Box 429, Geneva, 44041-0429	(216) 466-8400	(216) 466-1724
Grand Lake St. Marys	Auglaize/Mercer	2	$25	X	X	X	-	-	X	X	X	UNL	834 Edgewater Drive, St. Marys 45885-0308	(419) 394-3611	(419) 394-2774
Harrison Lake	Fulton	3	$27	X	X	X	-	3	X	X	X	EMO	Route #1, Box 240, Fayette, 43521-9751	(419) 237-2593	(419) 237-2332
Hocking Hills	Hocking	3†	$27	X	X	X	-	24	§	-	-	—	20160 S.R. 664, Logan, 43138-9537	(614) 385-6841	(614) 385-8166
Hueston Woods	Preble/Butler	3†	$25	X	X	X	-	10	X	X	X	10hp	Route #1, College Corner, 45003-9625	(513) 523-6347	(513) 523-7484
Indian Lake	Logan	2	$25	X	X	X	▲2	7	X	N	X	UNL	12774 S.R. 235 N., Lakeview, 43331-9217	(513) 843-2717	(513) 843-4450
Jackson Lake	Jackson	-	-	X	-	-	▲1	-	X	-	X	10hp	P.O. Box 174, Oak Hill, 45656-0174	(614) 682-6197	(614) 682-7098
Jefferson Lake	Jefferson	2	$20	-	-	-	-	15	X	-	X	EMO	R.D. 1, Box 140, Richmond, 43944-9710	(614) 765-4459	(614) 765-5698
Kelleys Island	Erie	2	$24	-	X	X	-	5	X	-	X	◆	4049 E. Moore's Dock Rd., Port Clinton, 43452-9708	(419) 797-4530	(419) 797-4025
Kiser Lake	Champaign	2	$20	-	-	-	-	4.5	X	X	X	NM	P.O. Box 55, Rosewood, 43070-0055	(513) 362-3822	(513) 362-9806
Lake Alma	Vinton	1	$23	X	-	-	-	2.5	X	X	X	EMO	Route #1, Box 422, Wellston, 45692-9801	(614) 384-4474	(614) 384-4473
Lake Hope	Vinton	3	$20	-	X	-	-	15	X	X	X	EMO	27331 S.R. 278, Box 3000, McArthur, 45651-8220	(614) 596-5253	(614) 596-4860
Lake Loramie	Auglaize/Shelby	4	$25	X	X	X	-	8	X	N	X	UNL	11221 S.R. 362, Minster, 45865-9311	(513) 295-2011	(513) 295-2119
Maumee Bay	Lucas	3†	$27	X	X	X	-	12	X	X	-	EMO /◆	1400 Park Rd. #1, Oregon, 43618-9777	(419) 836-7758	(419) 836-8711
Mohican	Ashland/Richland	-	-	X	X	X	▲2	12	§	-	X	—	3116 S.R. 3, Loudonville, 44842-9526	(419) 994-4290	(419) 994-3477
Mount Gilead	Morrow	4	$24	X	X	X	-	3.5	-	X	X	EMO	4119 S.R. 95, Mt. Gilead, 43338-9586	(419) 946-1961	(419) 946-1242
Paint Creek	Highland/Ross	3	$24	X	X	X	■1	8	X	X	X	UNL	14265 U.S. Rte. 50, Bainbridge, 45612-9503	(513) 365-1401	(513) 365-1986
Punderson	Geauga	4	$26	X	X	X	-	14	X	X	X	EMO	P.O. Box 338, Newbury, 44065-9684	(216) 564-2279	(216) 564-7542
Pymatuning	Ashtabula	3	$25	X	X	X	-	3	X	X	X	10hp	P.O. Box 1000, Andover, 44003-1000	(216) 293-6329	(216) 293-5384
Rocky Fork	Highland	4†	$26	X	X	X	-	4	X	X	X	UNL	9800 N. Shore Drive, Hillsboro, 45133-9205	(513) 393-4284	(513) 393-4287
Salt Fork	Guernsey	3	$24	X	X	X	-	14	X	X	X	UNL	14755 Cadiz Road, Lore City, 43755-9602	(614) 439-3521	(614) 432-1515
Shawnee	Scioto	3†	$24	X/-	X	X	-	5	X	X	X	EMO /◆	4404 S.R. 125, Portsmouth, 45663-9003	(614) 858-4561	(614) 858-6677
Stonelick	Clermont	5	$25	X	X	X	-	7	X	-	X	EMO	2895 Lake Drive, Pleasant Plain, 45162-9613	(513) 625-7544	(513) 625-7526
Strouds Run	Athens	3	$20	-	-	-	-	16	X	X	X	10hp	11661 State Park Road, Athens, 45701-9781	(614) 592-2302	(614) 594-7805
West Branch	Portage	2	$22	-	-	-	-	12.5	X	X	X	UNL	5708 Esworthy Road, Ravenna, 44266-9659	(330) 296-3239	(330) 296-0638

▲ Tepee ■ RV ♦ Houseboat † One or more units wheelchair accessible EMO - Electric motors only NM - No motors permitted UNL - Unlimited Horsepower
● Coin operated ●● Jet ski rental only § Swimming pool N - Nearby 10hp - 10 horsepower limit ◆ - Access to Lake Erie or Ohio River (UNL)

Application for Reservation

	Daytime phone ( )	For Office Use Only	
(PLEASE PRINT) Name		Deposit received:	Amount:
Address (street, city, state, zip)	# of sites desired # of persons in party		Receipt #:
Select option below and indicate park choice and preferred check in and check out dates in blanks provided	First choice (name of park) Check in date: Check out date:	Notice Mailed:	
☐ Rent-A-Camp (Indicate park at right) ☐ Rent-A-RV (Alum Creek or East Fork)	Second choice (name of park) Check in date: Check out date:	Reservation:	
☐ Rent-A-Tepee (Indian Lake, Jackson Lake, Mohican) ☐ Rent-A-Houseboat (Paint Creek)	Third choice (name of park) Check in date: Check out date:	Arrival:	Departure:

☐ Please check here if you are eligible for a Golden Buckeye Card or Veterans Administration discount.

Restful bank fishing is a few steps from Rent-A-Camp sites at Lake Loramie.

Ohio State Camping Parks

Alum Creek - (614) 548-4631
3615 South Old State Road
Delaware, OH 43015
Water, 3,387 acres
Land, 5,213 acres
Swimming beach
297 campsites with electric

A.W. Marion - (614) 869-3124
7317 Warner-Huffer Road
Circleville, OH 43113
Water, 146 acres
Land, 308 acres
Swimming beach
60 campsites, no electric

Barkcamp (614) 484-4064
65330 Barkcamp Park Road
Belmont, OH 43718
Water, 117 acres
Land, 1,232 acres
Swimming beach
150 campsites, no electric
Beaver Creek (330) 385-3091
Route 1

12021Echo Dell Road
East Liverpool, OH 43920
River and land, 3,038 acres
55 campsites, no electric

Blue Rock (614) 674-4794
7924 Cutler Lake Road
Blue Rock, OH 43720
Water, 15 acres
Land, 335 acres
Swimming beach
101 campsites, no electric

Buck Creek (937) 322-5284
1901 Buck Creek Lane
Springfield, OH 45502
Water, 2,120
Land, 1,910
Swimming beach, cabins
89 campsites with electric
12 no electric
Burr Oak - (614) 767-3570
Route 2, Box 286
Glouster, OH 45732
Water, 664 acres

Land, 2,592 acres
Swimming beach,
113 campsites, no electric
Burr Oak Lodge, Cabins - 1-800-282-7275

Caesar Creek (937) 897-3055
8570 East State Route 73
Waynesville, OH 45068
Water, 2,830 acres
Land, 7,941 acres
Swimming beach
287 campsites, electric

Cowan Lake (937) 289-2105
729 Beechwood Road
Wilmington, OH 45177
Water, 700 acres
Land, 1,075 acres
Swimming beach
237 campsites, electric

Deer Creek (614) 869-3124

20635 Waterloo Road
Mt. Sterling, OH 43143
Water, 1,277 acres
Land, 3,617 acres
Swimming beach
232 campsites, electric
golf course - (614) 869-3088
lodge, cabins - 1-800-282-7275

Delaware (614) 369-2761
5202 U.S. 23 North
Delaware, OH 43015
Water, 1,330 acres
Land, 1,815 acres
Swimming beach
164 campsites, with electric
 50 campsites, without electric

Dillon - (614) 453-4377
5265 Dillon Hills Drive
P.O. Box 126
Nashport, OH 43830
Water, 1,660 acres
Land, 6,030 acres
Swimming beach
183 campsites, with electric
12 campsites, no electric

East Fork (513) 734-4323
P.O. Box 119
Bethel, OH 45106
Water, 2,160 acres
Land, 8,420 acres
Swimming beach
416 campsites, with electric

East Harbor - (419) 734-5857
1169 North Buck Road
Lakeside-Marblehead, OH 43440
On Lake Erie
Land, 1,152 acres
Swimming beach
570 campsites, no electric

Findley - (216) 647-4490
25381 State Route 58
Wellington, OH 44090
Water, 93 acres
Land, 903 acres
Swimming beach

272 campsites, no electric

Forked Run - (614) 378-6206
P.O. Box 127
Reedsville, Ohio 45772
Water - 102 acres
Land - 815 acres
Swimming beach
198 campsites; no electric

Geneva - (216) 466-8400
Padanarum Road, Box 429,
Geneva, OH 44041
On Lake Erie
Land, 698 acres
Swimming beach
156 campsites, no electric
50 with electric

**Grand Lake St. Marys -
(419) 394-3611**
834 Edgewater Dr.
St. Marys Ohio 45885
Water, 13,500 acres
Land - 500 acres
Swimming beach
135 with electricity
71 without electric

**Guilford Lake -
(216)-222-1712**
6835 E. Lake Road
Lisbon, Ohio 44432
Water - 396 acres
Land - 92 acres
Swimming beach
42 campsites, no electric

**Harrison Lake -
(419) 237-2593**
Rt. 1, Box 240, Fayette, OH 43521
Water - 105 acres
Land - 142 acres
Swimming beach
126 campsites with electric
67 campsites, no electric

**Hocking Hills -
(614) 385-6841**
20160 State Route 664

Logan Ohio 43138
Water - 17 acres
Land - 2,000 acres
159 campsites,with electric
13 campsites, no electric

**Hueston Woods -
(513) 523-6347**
Rt. #1, College Corner,
Ohio 45003
Water, 625 acres
Land, 2,971 acres
Swimming beach
255 campsites, with electric
236 campsites, no electric
Golf Course - (513) 523-8081
Hueston Wood Lodge, Cabins -
1-800-282-7275

**Independence Dam -
(419) 784-3263**
Defiance, Ohio 43512
27722 S.R. 424 On the river
Land - 604 acres
40 campsites, no electric

Indian Lake - (513) 843-271
12774 State Route 235 North
Lakeview, OH 43331
Water - 5,800 acres
Land - 652 acres
Swimming beach
370 campsites, with electric
73 campsites, no electric

**Jackson Lake -
(614) 682-6197**
P.O. Box 174, Oak Hill, OH 4565
Water, 242 acres
Land, 92 acres
Swimmig beach
34 campsites, electric

**Jefferson Lake -
(614) 765-4459**
Rt.#1, Box 140, Richmond, OH
43944
Water, 17 acres
Land, 944 acres

Swimming beach
97 campsites, no electric

John Bryan - (937) 767-1274
3790 State Route 370
Yellow Springs, OH 45387
On the river
Land, 750 acres
100 campsites, no electric

**Kelleys Island -
(419) 797-4530**
On Lake Erie
Land, 661 acres
Swimming beach
129 campsites, no electric

Kiser Lake - (937) 362-3822
P.O. Box 55
Rosewood, OH 43070
Water, 396 acres
Land, 474 acres
Swimming beach, 115 campsites,
no electric

Lake Alma - (614) 384-4474
P. O. Box 42, Wellston, Ohio
45692
Water, 60 acres
Land, 290 acres
Swimming beach
80 campsites, with electric

**Lake Erie Islands
(419) 797-4530**
All reservation information
for Catawba, South Bass and
Kelleys Island -
4049 E. Moore's Dock Road
Port Clinton, OH 43452.

Lake Hope -(614) 596-5253
P.O. Box 279, Zaleski, OH 45698
Water, 120 acres
Land, 3,103 acres
Swimming beach
46 campsites, with electric
77 campsites, no electric

**Lake Loramie -
(937) 295-2011**
11211 St. Rt. 362, Minster, OH
45865
Water, 1,655 acres
Land, 400 acres
Swimming beach
132 campsites, with electric
32 campsites, no electric

Lake White - (614) 947-4059
2767 State Route 551
Waverly, OH 45690
Water, 337 acres
Land, 92 acres
23 campsites, no electric

Malabar - (419) 892-2784
4050 Bromfield Road
Lucas, OH 44843
Water, 3 acres
Land, 914 acres
15 campsites, no electric

**Mary Jane Thurston -
(419) 832-7662**
I-466, State Route 65
McClure, OH 43534
On the river
Land, 555 acres
31 campsites, no electric

**Maumee Bay -
(419) 836-7758**
1400 Park Road #1
Oregon, OH 43618
On Lake Erie
Land - 1,350 acres
Swimming beach, cabins, lodge
256 campsites, with electric
Maumee Bay, lodge, cabins -
1-800-282-7275

Mohican -(419) 994-4290
3116 State Route 3
Loudonville, OH 44842
On the river
Land, 1,294
153 campsites, with electric

24 campsites, no electric
Mohican Lodge Reservations,
Cabin, 1-800-282-7275

**Mosquito Lake -
(216) 637-2856**
1439 State Route 305
Cortland, OH 44410
Water - 7,850 acres
Land - 3,961 acres
Swimming beach
234 campsites, no electric

**Mount Gilead -
(419) 946-1961**
4119 State Route 95
Mt. Gilead, OH 43338
Water, 32 acres
Land - 140 acres
60 campsites, with electric

**Muskingum River Parkway -
(614) 452-3820**
P.O. Box 2806
Zanesville, OH 43702
On the river
Land, 120 acres
20 campsites, no electric

Paint Creek - (937) 365-1401
14265 U.S. Route 50
Bainbridge, OH 45612
Water, 1,200 acres
Land - 9,000 acres
Swimming beach
199 campsites with electric

Pike Lake - (614) 493-2212
1847 Pike Lake Road
Bainbridge, OH 45612
Water, 13 acres
Land - 600 acres
Swimming beach, cabins
101 campsites, with electric
11 campsites, no electric

**Portage Lakes -
(330) 644-2220**
5031 Manchester Road

Akron, OH 44319
Water, 2,520 acres
Land,- 1,000 acres
Swimming beach
74 campsites, no electric

Punderson - (216) 564-2279
P.O. Box 338, Newbury, OH
44065
Water, 150 acres
Land - 846 acres
Swimming beach, cabins, lodge
Reservations - 1-800-282-7275
201 campsites with electric
Golf Course - (216) 564-5465

Pymatuning -
(216) 293-6329
P.O. Box 1000,
Andover, OH 44003
Water, 14,000 acres
Land, 3,500 acres
Swimming beach
352 campsites, with electric
21 campsites, no electric

Rocky Fork - (937) 393-4284
9800 N. Shore Drive
Hillsboro, OH 45133
Water, 2,080 acres
Land, 1,384 acres
Swimming beach
137 campsites, with electric
40 campsites, no electric

Salt Fork - (614) 439-3521
14755 Cadiz Road
Lore, City, OH 43755
Water, 2,952 acres
Land - 17,229 acres
Swimming beach
212 campsites with electric
Salt Fork Lodge, cabins,
1-800-282-7275
Golf Course - (614) 432-7185

Scioto Trail - (614) 663-2125
144 Lake Road,
Chillicothe, OH 45601
Water - 30 acres

Land - 218 acres
20 campsites, with electric
57 campsites, no electric

Shawnee - (614) 858-4561
Star Route, Box 68
Portsmouth, OH 45663
Water, 68 acres
Land - 1,100 acres
Swimming beach
104 campsites with electric
3 campsites, no electric
Shawnee Lodge, cabins - 1-800-
282-7275
Golf Course - (614)858-6681

South Bass Island
See Lake Erie Islands
Land, 35 acres
135 campsites, no electric

Stonelick - (513) 625-7544
2895 Lake Drive
Pleasant Plain, OH 45162
Water, 200 acres
Land - 1,058 acres
Swimming beach
115 campsites with electric

Strouds Run - (614) 592-
2302
11661 State Park Road
Athens, OH 45701
Water, 161 acres
Land, 2,445 acres

Swimming beach
80 campsites, no electric

Tar Hollow - (614) 887-4818
16396 Tar Hollow Road
Laurelville, OH 43135
Water, 15 acres
Land - 619 acres
Swimming beach
28 campsites, with electric
47 campsites, no electric

Van Buren - (419) 299-3461
P.O. Box 117, Van Buren, OH
45889
Water, 45 acres
Land - 251 acres
40 campsites, no electric

West Branch -
(330) 296-3239
5708 Esworth Road, Route #5
Ravenna, OH 44266
Water, 2,650 acres
Land, 5,352 acres
Swimming beach
103 campsites, no electric

Wolf Run - (614) 732-5035
16170 Wolf Run Road
Caldwell, OH 43724
Swimming beach
Water, 220 acres
Land, 1,118 acres
140 campsites, no electric

Alum Creek campsites afford beautiful views right
from your tent.

Camping Park Directory

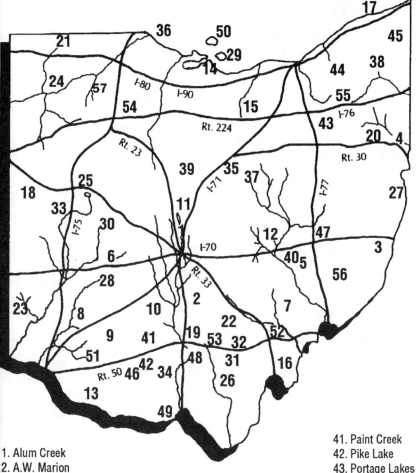

1. Alum Creek
2. A.W. Marion
3. Barkcamp
4. Beaver Creek
5. Blue Rock
6. Buck Creek
7. Burr Oak
8. Caesar Creek
9. Cowan Lake
10. Deer Creek
11. Delaware
12. Dillon
13. East Fork
14. East Harbor
15. Findley
16. Forked Run

17. Geneva
18. Grand Lake
    St. Marys
19. Great Seal
20. Guilford Lake
21. Harrison Lake
22. Hocking Hills
23. Hueston Woods
24. Independence Dam
25. Indian Lake
26. Jackson Lake
27. Jefferson Lake
28. John Bryan

57. Mary Jane Thurston

29. Kelleys Island
30. Kiser Lake
31. Lake Alma
32. Lake Hope
33. Lake Loramie
34. Lake White
35. Malabar
36. Maumee Bay
37. Mohican
38. Mosquito Lake
39. Mount Gilead
40. Muskingum River

41. Paint Creek
42. Pike Lake
43. Portage Lakes
44. Punderson
45. Pymatuning
46. Rocky Fork
47. Salt Fork
48. Scioto Trail
49. Shawnee
50. South Bass
    Island
51. Stonelick
52. Strouds Run
53. Tar Hollow
54. Van Buren
55. West Branch
56. Wolf Run

153

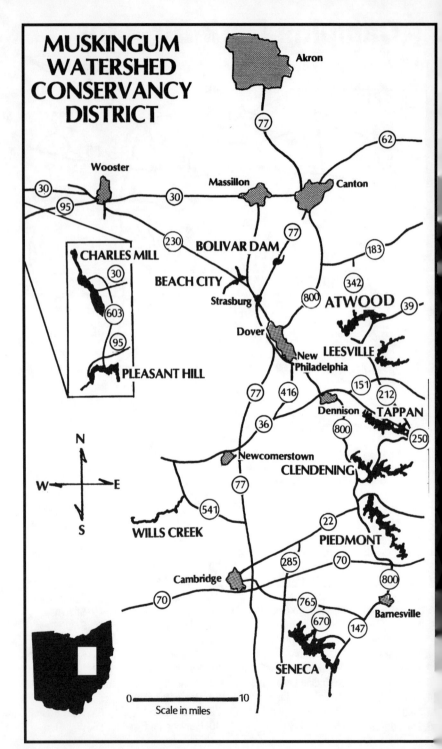

MUSKINGUM WATERSHED CONSERVANCY DISTRICT

Akron

77

62

Wooster

30

Massillon

Canton

30

95

230

BOLIVAR DAM

77

183

CHARLES MILL

30

BEACH CITY

342

603

Strasburg

800

ATWOOD

95

Dover

39

PLEASANT HILL

New Philadelphia

LEESVILLE

77

416

151

212

36

Dennison

TAPPAN

800

250

Newcomerstown

CLENDENING

N

W E

S

77

541

22

WILLS CREEK

PIEDMONT

285

70

Cambridge

800

70

765

670

147

Barnesville

SENECA

0 —————— 10
Scale in miles

Conservancy District information

LAKE RECREATION AREAS	ACRES (Water - Land)	Address	Baits & Tackle	Boat Rental	Boat Docks	Camping	Cabins (C) Motel (M)	Food Service	Swimming	Picnicking	Maximum Motor Horsepower
Atwood Lake — ATWOOD LAKE PARK (330) 343-6780; ATWOOD LAKE LODGE; ATWOOD MARINA (216) (330) 364-4703; DELLROY MARINA (216) (330) 735-2323	1540 / 2996	Mineral City, Ohio 44656; Dellroy, Ohio 44620; Mineral City, Ohio 44656; Dellroy, Ohio 44620	X X	X X	X X	X	C C M	X X X X	X X	X	25 H.P.
Beach City Lake	420 / 930	Beach City, Ohio 44608				X	M	X		X	10 H.P.
Charles Mill Lake — CHARLES MILL LAKE PARK (419) 368-6885; CHARLES MILL MARINA (419) 368-5951	1350 / 1997	Mansfield, Ohio 44903; Mansfield, Ohio 44903	X	X	X	X		X			10 H.P.
Clendening Lake — CLENDENING MARINA (614) 658-3691	1800 / 4750	Freeport, Ohio 43973	X	X	X	X	C	X			10 H.P.
Leesville Lake — Clow's MARINA (614) 269-5371; PETERSBURG MARINA (330) 627-4270	1000 / 2627	Bowerston, Ohio 44695; Carrollton, Ohio 44615	X X	X X	X X	X X	C C	X X			10 H.P.
Piedmont Lake — PIEDMONT MARINA (614) 658-3735	2270 / 4372	Freeport, Ohio 43973	X	X	X	X	M	X			10 H.P.
Pleasant Hill Lake — PLEASANT HILL LAKE PK. (419) 938-7884; PLEASANT HILL MARINA (419) 938-6488	850 / 1345	Perrysville, Ohio 44864; Perrysville, Ohio 44864	X	X	X	X	C	X X	X	X	Unlimited
Seneca Lake — SENECA LAKE PARK (614) 685-6013; SENECA MARINA POINT; SENECA MARINA (614) 685-5831	3550 / 4063	Senecaville, Ohio 43780; Senecaville, Ohio 43780; Senecaville, Ohio 43780	X	X	X	X X X	C	X X	X	X	180 H.P.
Tappan Lake — TAPPAN LAKE PARK (614) 922-3649; TAPPAN MARINA (614) 269-2031	2350 / 5026	Deersville, Ohio 44693; Scio, Ohio 43988	X	X	X	X X	C C	X	X	X	120 H.P.
Wills Creek Lake	900 / 4846	Coshocton, Ohio 43812									10 H.P.

More information about the lakes, cabins, campgrounds and other facilities can be obtained by writing: Recreation Department, Muskingum Watershed Conservancy District, 1319 Third St. N.W., P.O. Box 349, New Philadelphia, Ohio 44663.

(Continued from page 8)

Dozens of outstanding streams flowing into the Ohio River provide some of the top bass fishing along this great waterway. Anglers on the tributaries were not interviewed.

Most Ohio fishermen trailer their boats to their favorite fishing spots. The Ohio River has numerous launching ramps, and many of them are listed in this guide under Lake Erie - Ohio River Ramps.

Schell says that from his observations, and his own fishing experience, his two favorite pools for bass fishing are the Pike Island Pool near Wheeling, W.V. and the Hannibal Pool near New Martinsville, W.V.

Saugers, hybrid striped bass and white bass usually are concentrated in the vicinity of the locks and dams.

Special fishing regulations apply to the sections of the river Ohio shares with Kentucky and West Virginia. At the Ohio-Kentucky sector, the regulations are daily limits of 6 and a 12-inch minimum size; 10 sauger, walleye or saugeye; 30 white, striped bass or hybrid striped bass; 2 muskies; 30 crappies. No minimum size limit applies to spotted bass.

At the Ohio-West Virginia sector, the daily limit is 6 bass, with no size limit; 10 sauger, walleye or saugeye; no limit on striped, hybrid striped bass or white bass, but no more than four of them can be over 15 inches; 2 muskies with a 30-inch minimum size limit and 2 northern pike with a 28-inch minimum size.

Ohio has an agreement with West Virginia. A license from either state allows you to fish both sides of the river. No such deal has been made with Kentucky. Anglers with an Ohio license must fish Ohio waters.

Better bass fishing has prompted tournament organizers to hold more events on the Ohio River.

Charter boat renting on Lake Erie
.... *Continued from Page 32*

For example, does the fee include bait, tackle and ice? Usually, it does not include tackle, nor does it include bait when soft craws are purchased for smallmouth bass fishing.

If the charter is for a full day and your party limits on walleyes, will the captain lead you to smallmouth bass or some other kind of fishing?

One final tip: Call the skipper the night before to make sure everything is in order. That could prevent a wasted drive to find out the trip has been called off because of bad weather.

Many anglers who cannot put together a group of four or six anglers for a party boat often go alone, or with a friend, and fish from a party boat. These boats run out of Port Clinton from Drawbridge, Pier One, Lakeside, Tipples Marina on Marblehead and at other locations east to Cleveland, and beyond.

Fishing with a group of 12 to 30 anglers can be fun, and sometimes productive if the captain can position his boat over the right spot. The party boats are not as fast as the sport-fishing boats and the captains cannot be expected to cover as much territory.

Party boats offer an economic advantage. The cost per person runs from $25 to $35 per day, and it may be less for seniors on weekdays.

The vast majority of the established charter boat skippers operate from marinas in the Western Basin, although a growing number of captains are working the Central Basin.

The easiest way to make contact with a charter boat operator is meeting fishing guides at sport shows, visiting the larger marinas where captains dock their boats, get in touch with the Chamber of Commerce in the area where you plan to fish, or contact the Lake Erie Charter Boat Association.

Bureaus in the heart of the Lake Erie fishing area:

Erie County Visitors Bureau,
231 Washington Row, Sandusky, Ohio 44870. Phone 1-800-255-3743.
Lorain County Visitors Bureau,
611 Broadway, Lorain, Ohio 44052. Phone 1-800-344-1673.
Ottawa County Visitors Bureau,
109 Madison Street, Port Clinton, Ohio 43452. Phone 1-800-441-1271, or 419-734-4386.
Sandusky County Visitors Bureau,
1510 East State Street, P.O. Box 643, Fremont, Ohio 43402.
Phone 1-800-255-8070.

Walleyes roared back at Lake Erie after Walt Seifert, Columbus, and other sport fishermen won the fight to stop commercial netting.

Keep a log

My best fishing tip has been saved for last.

Get a calendar and start scheduling your fishing trips. And don't be deterred from the sport that gives you so much pleasure.

Too many people begin the year saying they intend to do a lot of fishing and end the season with the comment," I never got around to it. Where did this year go?"

When you do go fishing, may I suggest that you keep a log of your trips, noting the date, location, temperature, wind, number of fish caught and other important factors.

Next winter, when the wind is howling, the snow is falling and you're hunched up by the fireplace, it'll be fun to review the log and make plans for another season. The notes you've kept will help you become a more successful angler.

Fishing Log

Date: _____ Location: _____

Fish Caught: _____ Temp.: _____ Wind: _____

Comments: _____

_____

Date: _____ Location: _____

Fish Caught: _____ Temp.: _____ Wind: _____

Comments: _____

_____

Date: _____ Location: _____

Fish Caught: _____ Temp.: _____ Wind: _____

Comments: _____

_____

Date: _____ Location: _____

Fish Caught: _____ Temp.: _____ Wind: _____

Comments: _____

_____

Date: _____ Location: _____

Fish Caught: _____ Temp.: _____ Wind: _____

Comments: _____

_____

Date: _____ Location: _____

Fish Caught: _____ Temp.: _____ Wind: _____

Comments: _____

_____

Date: _____ Location: _____

Fish Caught: _____ Temp.: _____ Wind: _____

Comments: _____

_____

Date: _____ Location: _____

Fish Caught: _____ Temp.: _____ Wind: _____

Comments: _____

_____

Date: _____ Location: _____

Fish Caught: _____ Temp.: _____ Wind: _____

Comments: _____

_____

Date: _____ Location: _____

Fish Caught: _____ Temp.: _____ Wind: _____

Comments: _____

_____

Date: _____ Location: _____

Fish Caught: _____ Temp.: _____ Wind: _____

Comments: _____

_____

Date: _____ Location: _____

Fish Caught: _____ Temp.: _____ Wind: _____

Comments: _____

_____

Date: _____ Location: _____

Fish Caught: _____ Temp.: _____ Wind: _____

Comments: _____

_____

Date: _____ Location: _____

Fish Caught: _____ Temp.: _____ Wind: _____

Comments: _____

_____

Date: _____ Location: _____

Fish Caught: _____ Temp.: _____ Wind: _____

Comments: _____

_____

Date: _____ Location: _____

Fish Caught: _____ Temp.: _____ Wind: _____

Comments: _____

_____

Date: _____ Location: _____

Fish Caught: _____ Temp.: _____ Wind: _____

Comments: _____

_____

Date: _____ Location: _____

Fish Caught: _____ Temp.: _____ W

Comments: _____

_____

Date: _____ Location: _____

Fish Caught: _____ Temp.: _____ Wind: _____

Comments: _____

_____

Date: _____ Location: _____

Fish Caught: _____ Temp.: _____ Wind: _____

Comments: _____

_____

Date: _____ Location: _____

Fish Caught: _____ Temp.: _____ Wind: _____

Comments: _____

_____

Date: _____ Location: _____

Fish Caught: _____ Temp.: _____ Wind: _____

Comments: _____

_____

Date: _____ Location: _____

Fish Caught: _____ Temp.: _____ Wind: _____

Comments: _____

_____

Date: _____ Location: _____

Fish Caught: _____ Temp.: _____ Wind: _____

Comments: _____

_____

━━━

Date: _____ Location: _____

Fish Caught: _____ Temp.: _____ Wind: _____

Comments: _____

_____

━━━

Date: _____ Location: _____

Fish Caught: _____ Temp.: _____ Wind: _____

Comments: _____

_____

━━━

Date: _____ Location: _____

Fish Caught: _____ Temp.: _____ Wind: _____

Comments: _____

_____

━━━

Date: _____ Location: _____

Fish Caught: _____ Temp.: _____ Wind: _____

Comments: _____

_____

━━━

Dedication

To my wife, Donna, a school teacher who never gave me
high marks for yard work, and who never once complained
when she heard me say, "I'm goin' fishin'."